Human Destiny

Human Destiny

Some Problems for Catholic Philosophy

Joseph Owens, C.Ss.R.

The Catholic University of America Press
Washington, D.C.

Library of Congress Cataloging in Publication Data
Owens, Joseph.
  Human destiny.
  Bibliography: p. Includes index.
  1. Fate and fatalism—History. 1. Title.
BD411.O9 1985   129   84-21496
ISBN 0-8132-0604-9
ISBN 0-8132-0605-7 (pbk.)

Such a life, of course, would be above that of a man, for a man will live in this manner not insofar as he is a man, but insofar as he has something divine in him.

ARISTOTLE, *E N*, 10.7, 1177b26–28; Apostle trans.

We know that in order to be fully human man must transcend himself and seek the ultimate reality and meaning of life. This was the witness of a Yyi Ch'adon in your own heritage.

JOHN PAUL II (in Korea), *Origins*, 14 (1984): 3.

TABLE OF CONTENTS

Introduction

The problems of human destiny, very much alive in the broad interests of concerned people today, can hardly help but call for minute scrutiny on the part of a Catholic philosopher. The third question of Immanuel Kant (*KRV,* B833), posed for both speculative and practical reason, was "What may I hope for?" Like a haunting specter, this query rises full-blown out of the pain and struggle and disappointments of both public and private human living. It confronts Catholic philosophy as inevitably and as poignantly as it does any other comprehensive type of serious humanistic thinking, for it has troubling philosophical facets. It is especially urgent at the present moment. In recent months widespread and forceful demonstrations on nuclear arms proliferation have given voice to a deeply felt grass-roots fear. Humanity, it would seem, is destining itself to a suicidal end in a worldwide atomic holocaust. Consequent change and poisoning of our entire atmosphere would result from the fallout complications. The nations of the world would seem to be treading their own death march.[1]

In another arena, similarly, ecologists speak about the greenhouse belt surrounding our planet because of industrial pollution, threatening the temperature required for human life. In still broader perspective physicists and astronomers track the remorseless change on planets and stars that is bringing to a gradual but inescapable terminus the mean required for vital processes. In a different and manageable area Marxist voices proclaim the disappearance of religion and the triumph of an economically regulated paradise. These voices are somewhat less strident now than they were in the earlier decades of the century, on account of practical troubles. Yet they are still politically strong and tirelessly persistent. Likewise other ideologies, perhaps less severe and less devastating but nonetheless based upon human ideas in accord with the standard notion of an ideology, would in one way or another make our well-being culminate in the bloom of a temporal prosperity enjoyed during earthly life.[2] In these views man's destiny does not extend beyond the presently experienced bodily existence.

On the other hand, in the dominant Judeo-Christian and Islamic traditions people are believed to be destined for a happiness merited through a God-centered life on earth but which is attained after bodily death. Even in Western pagan traditions an ingrained belief in survival has played a striking role, as in Greek doctrines of transmigration of souls or in the Nordic conception of a Valhalla. In the Platonic myths people were judged after death and apportioned reward or punishment in keeping with their deeds during earthly life. The ultimate destiny of human beings, according to these vivid representations, was to be found in an existence after the present lifetime. Some of the older pictures of a future state were gloomy, as in the concepts of Sheol, Hades, or Tartarus. Others were bright, as in Plato's *Phaedrus* (114C–115A) and *Republic* (X, 621CD). But regardless of the quality of the life, the location of human destiny in a future existence after bodily death has deep roots in Western culture.

Against this background, the question of human destiny has a lively interest for Catholic philosophy. Each Sunday the Catholic thinker professes publicly his belief in the almighty and triune God, whose fatherhood extends to all mankind, and whose special providence blossoms in the communion of saints and in the forgiveness of sins, as well as in the resurrection of the body and the consequent everlasting life. These articles of faith add considerable prospects of expansion to the answer for Kant's first question "What can I know?" In regard to Kant's second question, "What should I do?" the commandments from Mount Sinai reinforce and extend the prescriptions of traditional moral philosophy. For his third question, "What may I hope for?" the vague intimations of unaided human thought are definitely specified by revelation. The hope held out in Christian faith is for an everlasting life of beholding face-to-face the infinite beauty and inexhaustible riches of the triune God. It is a vision to be possessed in eternal security, and in a way that satisfies to the full the tendencies and desires of a soul elevated through supernatural grace.[3]

A Catholic philosopher, in consequence, approaches the question of human destiny with a view of it already held firmly through his faith. As long as he is remaining in the Catholic context, he cannot accept any real deviation from this basic conception. Nor can he be expected even for purposes of methodical procedure to abstract for the moment from his belief, in an effort to reason as though he had as yet no definite notion of what human destiny is. For he is not at all aiming at substitution of an alternative way through which acquaintance with man's destiny can be arrived at philosophically. He is in no way attempting to demonstrate by reason what can be known only through religious belief. Rather, what he accepts through faith about human destiny raises for him many queries that call for philosophical answers. In both the theoretical and the practical areas numerous items in the content of religious beliefs, both his own and those of others, prompt genuinely philosophical questions. The beliefs themselves take on the role of phenomena with aspects that come under the investigation of philosophy.

In this regard they require philosophical probing. The answers on those aspects are accordingly not matters of belief but conclusions reached on strictly philosophical premises.

Theoretical difficulties, for instance, lie in the question how contemplation, even though it be the vision of God, can satisfy all the legitimate aspirations of the human heart. A person naturally wants to act, to do real things. How can just beholding some object, even though it be the highest, be the sum total of what may be hoped for? How can contemplation alone be the ultimate destiny of so complicated and endowed a personality as that of a human being? How can mere intellection be a full life, an existential life, for a cognitive agent who delights in possessing things in their real existence rather than in what would seem to be a dream world of mere thought? How can love and interpersonal relations be maintained in the realm of pure contemplation? These and other difficult questions in the order of theoretical philosophy come to the fore when one faces the Christian doctrine of vision as the activity constituting the ultimate destiny of man. They quite obviously invite philosophical answers.

Similarly in the practical order acute philosophical problems have to be faced. A Catholic philosopher lives today in a world where only a minority shares his belief in what human destiny is and in the way it is to be attained. Yet frequent occasions arise in which this belief brings him into conflict with those who do not share it. Important matters of conduct in the areas of education, marriage, sexual morality, respect for human life, and the extent of civil authority will be at stake. In these matters the natural and the supernatural dimensions have to be brought into harmony. Full life in the communion of saints needs to be reconciled with full life in the national and international communities of mankind. But how can the doctrine of the forgiveness of sins be lived with any real meaning and effective cooperation in an atmosphere in which accountability to a supreme judge no longer prevails, and where people claim to be free to shape their morality according to their own individual preferences and conveniences? What is the relation of inherent human rights to a divine dominion known only through revelation? How can the instinctive claim that

> I am the master of my fate:
> I am the captain of my soul[4]

be maintained in the face of a destiny already prescribed by a divine will?

These are philosophical questions, to be probed and answered on the philosophical level. In the wake of Hume, Kant, and Hegel the philosophy of religion has become a recognized study.[5] It makes religion the object of philosophical investigation. It takes religious beliefs and experience as it finds them. It deals with them in various ways as phenomena, and among other tasks investigates their relations to different areas of human experience and reflection. It is not theology, for it is not proceeding from revealed principles to establish its conclusions. It keeps revealed tenets to the status of thematic objects for consideration. Nor is it moral philosophy, which aims to direct human conduct, and would give answers to Kant's second question. Still less is it located on the level of the particular or statistical sciences that bear upon special phases of its general subject matter. Its procedure is not based on qualitative or quantitative principles, as those sciences would require. It is strictly philosophical in its techniques, even though it is dealing with religious matters either immediately experienced or else deduced by theologians as conclusions from basic beliefs.

In admitting religious data and ensuing theological deductions into his thematic subject matter, the Catholic philosopher is in effect declining to accept the assumption that nature considered just by itself is a finished whole.[6] Principles based on nature continue to stand firm for him in their own right. No skeptical distrust in them is implied. But that does not mean that they tell the whole story even about nature itself. Hamlet's poetic intuition

> There are more things in heaven and earth, Horatio,
> Than are dreamt of in your philosophy (1.5.166–167)

may be taken as a profound insight based on real affectivity, and is deserving of respect. Nature does not always show itself as perfect, and may well need completing, even though when viewed just in itself it does not reveal the need of completion by grace. The possibility of supernatural completion can well be left open by philosophy, and when indicated by religion it can be discussed philosophically. Philosophy can well entertain that breadth of vision for its themes. It need not close its eyes to a whole area of human experience.

In a Catholic philosophical approach to a religious topic, therefore, naturally grounded knowledge retains its own unshakable truth. But naturally knowable truth need not be the whole truth even about nature. Rather, it is the account that would be complete if nature were a finished whole. Where tenets held on religious faith show that nature needs completion by grace, important theoretical and practical questions may be found only incompletely answered on the plane of unaided natural knowledge. Queries about human destiny are by no means the least among these. Confrontation with the supernatural dimension can in consequence raise a number of genuinely philosophical problems, with queries that belong to the *philosophy* of religion rather than just to sacred theology.

General though these considerations may be, they are best studied in particular situations. On the one hand there is the characteristically pagan situation, in which no explicit debt to formal revelation can be traced. This outlook is well exemplified in Aristotle of Stagira, the fourth-century B.C. Greek thinker whose moral teaching was brilliantly directed towards the achievement of the highest human happiness, and whose metaphysics culminated in the eternal and the divine. Yet no direct influence of Hebraic revelation upon his thought is demonstrable.

On the other hand the conception of human destiny may be examined in a culture deeply penetrated by biblical revelation, as in Jewish, Christian, or Islamic civilizations. In these surroundings the ultimate goal of human life was something accepted on religious faith. But philosophical inquiries concerning it were lively and penetrating. The attitude is exemplified in outstanding fashion in the works of St. Thomas Aquinas, in the thirteenth century A.D.

Thirdly, the question of human destiny may be faced as it emerges in the multicultural and geopolitical arena of today's civilization. Perhaps somewhat less than half the global population may at least nominally acknowledge the fact of formal divine revelation.[7] Yet the conceptions of its nature and content differ widely, and its overall influence on practical reasoning and public life can hardly be considered dominant. Pitted against it are numerous secularistic philosophies and ideological theories that seek to control human conduct in ways incompatible with it. The problem of coexistence accordingly comes to the fore.

The ensuing study, then, proposes to examine the question of human destiny first in the conception of it attained by unaided reasoning in Aristotle, secondly in the philosophical aspects of divinely revealed doctrine as interpreted by Aquinas, and thirdly in the coexistence of the revealed doctrine with currently prevalent trends.

CHAPTER ONE

Human Destiny in Aristotle

I

Aristotle's theoretical teaching, in its various ramifications, offers a clear and comprehensive philosophical answer to Kant's first question "What can I know?" Sensible things in the real world, it shows, are directly and immediately perceived in human cognition. Also, the percipient himself and his cognitive activity are thereby immediately attained, not directly, but only concomitantly. From these real and immediate objects of awareness are drawn conclusions that reach both the internal and external causes of sensible things and finally a supersensible order of being. The epistemological procedure is explained with remarkable acuteness and cogency. Cognition is tellingly assessed as a way of being, in which percipient and thing perceived become, and are, identical in the actuality of the awareness. In consequence there could not be awareness of the one without concomitant awareness of the other, and observation shows satisfactorily that in human cognition what is perceived directly is always something else, and that what is perceived concomitantly is the cognition itself. That is Aristotle's overall theoretical teaching.[1]

Further, Kant's second question, "What should I do?" was answered extensively in Aristotle's practical philosophy, handed down in three collections of ethical treatises.[2] Locating the first principle of conduct in choice, the Aristotelian ethics reasoned to the way choice is to be guided in conformity with its rational character.[3] The spontaneous appeal of rationally initiated conduct over the slavery of necessitated action was accepted gladly, and the complicated study for its correct guidance was undertaken in the treatises.

Immersed in this ethical procedure, which continually accepts purely theoretical conclusions for use as its instruments, is to be sought the Aristotelian answer to Kant's third question, "What may I hope for?" The problem is broached in the opening chapters of the *Nicomachean Ethics*. That work began with a factual statement of all-embracing range. Every human undertaking, it asserted, appears to aim at something good.[4] Aristotle claimed no originality for this observation. He wrote as though it were well known and accepted by everybody. It needed merely to be recalled for his listeners, without requirement of demonstration. Anyone, today as then, knows that people do not enter a course of action without something good as motive, even though the motive be just diversion or distraction. Aristotle (*E N*, 1.1,1094a6–18) gave as examples the health intended through medical care, a vessel through shipbuilding, victory through the waging of war, and wealth through the administration of estates. In these pursuits, he noted, one good was subordinated to another in being sought for its sake. But ultimately all were pursued for a single, overall good. Most people, he continued (1.4,1095a17–20), are quite in agreement in giving this supreme good the designation "happiness."

The Greek term used here by Aristotle for happiness was

eudaimonia. Etymologically it meant having a good *daimôn*, in the sense of divinely bestowed direction for one's life.[5] The word itself, therefore, carried the overtones of divine favor and guidance, somewhat as the Latin term *numen* implied the benevolent nod of the divinity. *Eudaimonia*, in consequence, was practically synonymous with the notion of having a good destiny.[6] It meant the genuine happiness implicitly sought by everyone in every rational action.

Yet the outright equating of the Aristotelian *eudaimonia* with human destiny calls for some nuancing. In ordinary use the Greek adjective *eudaimôn* tended to emphasize material and social prosperity. It meant flourishing.[7] But it could also be used synonymously with *makarios*, an adjective that implied the bliss enjoyed by the gods.[8] It was accordingly wide open to a spiritual connotation. Still it did not necessarily require that notion. Aristotle stressed the fact that the generality of people, most commonplace in tastes yet justifying their conduct by the sensual indulgence of many in high places, seem to choose a life of sensual pleasure for their happiness. It is a life for cattle, utterly slavish (*E N,* 1.5,1095b14–22). This motivation, when allowed to run its full course, lowers a person to the brute level and cuts off access to goods that are properly human. So dissolute a conception of *eudaimonia* can hardly be regarded as the destiny towards which human nature points in its dignity as human. Yet it is *chosen* by these people as their highest good.

Other persons who are cultured and of a practical bent, Aristotle goes on, choose prestige as their ultimate goal and happiness. But prestige, with all its fame and power in the glare of public life, is something fickle and deceptive. It is located in the whims of popular opinion, and it pursues the shadow rather than the substance of commendable action, for it sets its aim on the public recognition of excellence rather than on the excellence itself (*E N,* 1.5,1095b22–1096a4). Its notion of *eudai-*

monia is therefore too superficial to be the destiny that corresponds to the exigencies of a person's intellectual nature, even though it is so often chosen by educated and enterprising men.[9]

Then there is the life of theoretical contemplation, Aristotle continues (*E N,* 1.5,1096a4–5). It places the supreme good and happiness of mankind in intellectual activity carried on for its own sake. As the exercise of man's highest and characteristic function, this type of activity when bearing upon the best objects constitutes the happiness that fully meets the recognizable indications of human nature (1.7,1097b22–1098a20; 10.7,1177a12–1178a6). It is therefore the highest kind of human happiness (1178a8). It is what the man who has been properly brought up will come to regard as the *eudaimonia* for which he is meant by his nature. Without any nuancing whatsoever, this type of happiness may be equated with human destiny as indicated by the nature of man. It still has to be chosen, as does any other moral object for Aristotle. It is not necessitated by human nature. Alternatives, such as prestige or sensual pleasure, are presented for the choice. But if the choice is made according to the balanced indications of man's nature, it will espouse the life of theoretical contemplation. There is some natural good in the other alternatives, which makes each of them an instance of what is sought in every human undertaking in accord with the opening sentence of the *Nicomachean Ethics.* But the correct ultimate end and the kind of action that leads up to it are now specified as a definite kind of good, the morally good. With Aristotle the morally good goes under the designation of the *kalon,* the Greek term usually translated by "the beautiful." There is difficulty in conveying its moral force through any one word or expression in English. The phrase "the morally good" covers its range, but misses the glowing attractiveness that plays so vital a part in understanding its role in the present context. In spite of drawbacks, the English term "right" would appear to be the most practical translation even though against a puritanical background it might make the notion of morality seem grim and chilling rather than attractive like the beautiful.[10]

Aristotle does not claim that the alternatives he mentions for the choice are exhaustive. He lists sensual pleasure, prestige, and theoretical contemplation as the three most prominent types of life (*E N,* 1.5,1095b17–19). But he was well aware that money-making had been looked upon by many as the supreme purpose of human living. This was traditionally illustrated by the Pythagorean legend that some went to the games to compete for fame, others to make money by selling their wares, and still others to watch, just for the pleasure of watching.[11] Aristotle dismissed the money-making motif rather lightly, since the money is in actual fact desired for something further, whether for pleasure or prestige or intellectual pursuits. It is in consequence for him never an ultimate end, but always in itself a means (1.5,1096a5–7). He does not take into consideration any psychological twist by which a man may seem to make the accumulation of wealth the sole object of his life, far beyond any possible use or ulterior pleasure.[12] Nor does he tolerate the notion of people living just to do good in general, even though that conception was professed by close friends of his (1.6,1096a11–1097a14). He requires something particular as the good for which one lives. In regard to the life of prestige, moreover, he does not give a role to lust of power just for its own sake, as in the case of kingmakers or backroom politicians who sedulously avoid publicity.

These points, however, are minor and peripheral as regards the present interest. What they do serve to bring out is the function of *choice* in the theme of human destiny. A person's destiny, no matter how much it is indicated by his or her nature, is something that he or she freely chooses. It is moreover something particular. Though happiness is always the agent's ultimate purpose, the thing or action in which the happiness is to be found is in fact left to the individual person's discretion. This is in full accord with the Stagirite's general conception of the moral or practical order. The moral order originates in human choice, which is the first principle or source of conduct (*E N*, 6.2., 1139a31). No matter how necessitarian the flow of natural events may have been for Aristotle and a little later for the Stoics and the Epicureans, these Greek thinkers did not at all feel compelled to make human conduct fit into a rigid determinism. They accepted choice as an internally observed fact. The choice was not *determined* by antecedent causes, regardless of how great the influence these causes exercised upon it may have been.

So, while for Aristotle himself the principles of theoretical science were seen in the things directly confronting the human mind, the principles of practical science were located in the agent's choice.[13] With him there was no sociobiological tendency to reduce choice to nature through efforts to explain the decisions ultimately by natural causes. The origin of a new course of action was attributed emphatically to the human agent: "For where we are free to act we are also free to refrain from acting, and where we are able to say No we are also able to say Yes" (*E N*, 3.5, 1113b7–8; trans. Rackham). The freedom of choice was recognized, and the person's responsibility for the course chosen was acknowledged. In this way the Stagirite laid bare the reason why practical science could not be reduced to theoretical knowledge. The basic principles of each were different in kind. His explanation justified philosophically the general Greek tendency to accept freedom in conduct while at the same time maintaining a necessitarian conception of nature.

But choice is a function of a rational agent. It requires that alternatives be compared, that deliberation about them be possible, and that the responsibility of making the decision in accord with right reason be present.[14] In this perspective the notion of goodness, which the *Nicomachean Ethics* introduced as the object of every undertaking, becomes significantly specified for moral philosophy. It is no longer left in its all-embracing generality. Each alternative for a proposed course of action has some goodness to render it attractive. Sensual pleasure is attractive, prestige and power are attractive, contemplation is attractive. Each offers a basis in goodness for making it an object of choice. But the goodness that appeals to right reason is of a special kind. It is the *kalon,* the morally right. It carries intrinsically in its attraction the duty to act in accordance with it, the obligation to work it out in practical conduct.[15] For the *Nicomachean Ethics* (1.3,1094b14–15), in consequence, the object of moral philosophy is introduced as the *kala,* the things that are morally right and just. It is a special type of goodness within the all-embracing ambit of the good as such. It involves in itself the duty of acting rationally, and not haphazardly.

In this Aristotelian conception, then, the choice of human destiny *should* be made in accord with man's nature as rational. The Stagirite sees no contradiction here between obligation and freedom. In fact, the one entails the other. In the *Metaphysics* (12.10, 1075a18–23) Aristotle observes that in a household the freemen are the ones least permitted to act at random. They should freely orient their actions towards the common good of the household, while slaves and lower animals want to act according to the impulses of the moment. Choice and *order* go hand in hand with Aristotle. Choice, in fact, as a rational activity involves the duty of choosing according to right reason. Making the correct choice means acting like a freeman. To choose one's ultimate good on the basis of sensual pleasure is slavish. To choose power or fame or riches or money-making or just abstract goodness is irrational, for reason shows that none of these is ultimate in the order of final causality. To be completely free, both from slavery and from error, means to be habituated to choose what is morally good and to act according to right reason.

Human destiny, then, is for Aristotle something freely chosen, but implying choice in accordance with the dignity of human nature. It is in that context that a person remains the master of his own fate and the captain of his soul. It may be that reverses and physical disasters beyond his control, as (supra, n. 6) in the case of King Priam of Troy, prevent him from attaining full happiness. He will nevertheless keep pursuing the *kalon* or the morally good by enduring his misfortunes with patience and greatness of soul (*E N,* 1.10,1100b19–1101a8; cf. 9,1100a5–9). He will still be remaining on top, and deliberately choosing the moral goodness that shines through his life in spite of all its terrible sufferings and disappointments and trials. He still chooses the *kalon,* in accord with the dignity of a person endowed with the admirable gifts of intelligence and freedom, guiding himself according to right reason. It is a decision made in a freedom that is permeated with order. There is nothing haphazard about it. It is supremely rational. But ultimately it issues from choice.

II

Human destiny as Aristotle sees it is accordingly something chosen. In what is known today as "the free world," this notion should encounter little opposition. In contrast to totalitarian ideologies, the spirit of civil liberties permits the citizen to pursue his individually chosen destiny in any way that is not glaringly and proximately destructive of the order that makes liberty possible. But with regard to the type of happiness that Aristotle declares *should* be freely chosen, no such widespread agreement in the present-day mentality will be encountered. For Aristotle the supreme goal of both individual and political striving was, as already noted, theoretical contemplation. This conception can hardly be mentioned today without evoking the reaction that it is an ivory-tower phantasy utterly divorced from the realities of everyday practical life.

Yet it was precisely from the everyday activities in the Greek city-state that Aristotle developed his conception of moral goodness and its culmination in a life of thought. He commenced the *Nicomachean Ethics* with a look at the way those activities were subordinated one to another and ultimately to the supreme goal of attaining happiness. In them justice, courage, moderation, wisdom, and related virtues were continually sought. The greater part of the *Nicomachean Ethics* studied those virtues, along with their functioning in friendships, and saw how they grounded the notion of the *kalon,* namely the morally good. The *kalon* was recognized immediately in the virtuous activities by anyone who had been brought up correctly from early childhood. But it was not found as something already set up by nature. It had to be determined in each instance by the way a proposed action corresponded to correct moral habituation. That was why proper upbringing and education were all-important with Aristotle for the recognition of what is morally good. The virtuous mean was in every case set up by the wise man in accord with his moral habituation. From these immediately recognized instances of the *kalon* in everyday activity and in friendships its highest instance, the *kalliston,* was inferred and chosen. People formed their conception of the supreme good, Aristotle noted, on the basis of the type of life they lead.[16] If they became habituated towards sense pleasure only, they made indulgence of the senses their ultimate goal. If basically habituated towards a quest for fame and power, they chose prestige as their greatest good. But if brought up to a life of virtue, whose object is the *kalon,* they will choose as its highest instance the supreme goal that is most in accord with their nature as human. It will be what corresponds to the intellectual apex of their nature. The life of theoretical contemplation will be therefore the *kalliston (E N,* 1.8,1099a22–31), the primary and dominating instance of moral goodness. It will be the morally good person's choice, the choice made according to his nature as rational. The reason is that "the actuality of mind is life" (*Metaph.,* 12.7,1072b26–27), life at its highest and best.

The tenet that theoretical contemplation is the supreme human good, then, was reached by Aristotle not in ideological fashion, but on the basis of what he saw in everyday life in the Greek city-state. Nevertheless people today, just as then, encounter obstacles in regarding the notion as anything other than ivory-tower philosophy. From early years children grow up wanting to be things, a fireman, an astronaut, a hockey star, a movie queen, a mother, a doctor, or something else in really actual life. People want to do things, to have things. Nobody wants to spend life just thinking. This way of arguing, however, could hardly be expected to impress Aristotle. For him, to perceive or to know a thing meant to become and be that thing in a higher way than by material possession. Cognition was a way of being that transcended material limitations. Through cognition the soul was potentially all things, sensible things through perception, intelligible objects through intellection (*De an.,* 3.8,431b20–28). In the actuality of cognition it was united in the closest way possible to all the things it perceived or knew, things that were really other than itself. There was no better way of being other things, or of acquiring possession of them.

Today this Aristotelian teaching on cognition receives comparatively little notice (cf. supra, n. 1). But it was given deep study in the tradition of the Greek commentators, and in the

Islamic and Christian interpreters of the Middle Ages. It continued to receive development in Renaissance and in later Scholastic circles. Its basic insight, that to know a thing is to become and be it in a higher way than through material reception, had already been presented in sharp outlines by Aristotle.[17] One may feel immediately that there is something lacking in the way he himself sketches it. Being things just in thought can at first hearing seem like living in a dream world of bubbles that may fly very high but burst at once on any brush with solid reality. Yet at the same time one retains the impression in reading Aristotle that it cannot be that fatuous, and that the intuition is fundamentally sound. What Aristotle seems to take for granted in his writings is that cognitional existence is a higher kind than material existence. This may not appear absurd for all its instances, but it does run counter to the common sense feeling that existence in one's real self is preferable to existence in someone else's thought. This sentiment is universalized to all things, including the noncognitive. However, that point can be left for consideration against a later background that is other than Aristotelian.[18] For the moment, one may say that Aristotle's understanding of cognition allows theoretical contemplation to be interpreted as containing within itself every other individual good that a person could desire.

III

Yet even with this all-embracing *range* of cognition granted, the objection may still be urged from another angle. Intellection is only one activity in man. A human being, however, is too complicated and multifaceted an agent to be limited to just one way of grasping other things. The full person, the objection goes, is meant for much more varied activity. Scope is needed for emotions, appetites, and associations with others of one's kind. To place one's destiny in a single activity is sadly to mistake the amplitude of human nature. No matter how broadly intellection may range in its objects, it is still only one type of activity. To place human happiness in it alone is to exclude much else. Thinking, just in itself, does not satisfy a human being's desire, even though its objects may be limitless. That is the commonly voiced argument.[19]

A careful reading of the Aristotelian texts, nevertheless, dissipates this type of objection. For happiness Aristotle requires pleasure in the highest degree, respectable family origin, good health and appearance, proper nourishment and sustinence and leisure, good fortune, satisfactory family life and children, friendship and cooperation with others in the various forms of social and political organization, and a full lifespan, with sufficient wealth to provide for self and for association with other people (*E N*, 1.8,1098b9–11,1101b9; 10.7,1177a22–9,1179a13). These factors are all included in Aristotle's rounded-out picture of human destiny. Interpreters have to acknowledge that at least sometimes Aristotle positively requires all these things for the state of human happiness. But some claim that at other times he virtually excludes them, either through inconsistency in thought or through change of opinion at different stages of his life. However, nowhere is any of them explicitly dissociated by the Stagirite himself from inclusion in man's ultimate goal.

Commentators who find inconsistency in Aristotle's teaching from this angle leave out of consideration a basic norm for the interpretation of his text. It was a norm that proved difficult to express concisely in Greek, and continues to be difficult in modern languages. In English, however, it has been felicitously phrased as "focal meaning."[20] In the typical universal treated by logic the nature in question is found equally shared in each individual, so that each is severally one single object (*Metaph.*,

5.26,1023b29–32). Socrates, Plato, Plotinus are each severally "a man," and "a man" is predicated in turn of each. Human nature is found on equal footing in each of them. But there is another kind of universal predication in which the nature is found as a nature in a primary instance only, and in all other instances through reference to the primary instance.[21] It is illustrated by Aristotle through the examples of health and medicine. These call for some explanation.

The nature of health is found only in the correct disposition of a living organism. Food, exercise, country air are healthy not because they have the nature of health in themselves, but because they cause it in the living organism. Cooked spinach is anything but healthy in the sense of having in itself the vigor and the vitality of the living plant. It is only through reference to the health in the human being, a health it is supposed to cause, that cooked spinach can be called healthy. Similarly a color is healthy, not through anything intrinsic to the color itself, but because it is a sign of the health in the human body. All these secondary instances are considered healthy through focal bearing on the primary instance, the correct disposition of the human organism. The meaning of health is in this way focal, focal in regard to a nature that is found as a nature solely in the primary instance. Correspondingly medicine is a science or art in the physician's mind, while books, remedies, institutes are medical insofar as they bear upon the medical art which is not in them but in the practitioner's mind. In contrast, human nature is found intrinsically in each individual man or woman.

Focal meaning pervades Aristotle's metaphysics, philosophy of nature, and moral philosophy. Being, the object of metaphysics, is found as a nature with its requirements of complete actuality and permanence in immaterial being only. All other things have natures of their own, men, animals, plants, and metals, but are beings through reference to completely

actual and permanent substance. The highest instance of being
and of truth is in this way the cause of what is designated by
those terms in all the other instances (*Metaph.*, 2.1,993b24–
31). The meaning is accordingly focal for all the varying instances. Book Delta of the *Metaphysics* discusses a considerable
number of objects with focal meaning. But the book is not
meant to be a lexicon in the modern sense.[22] Actuality, for
instance, which is an important metaphysical object found in
perfect fashion in separate substance but imperfectly in mobile
things, is not listed. There need accordingly be no surprise that
an ethical notion such as the *kalon* is not included, even though
in a passage already noted (*E N,* 1.8,1099a22–31) its supreme
instance is called the *kalliston,* marking that instance the cause
of the *kalon* in all other instances. Moreover, just as the primary
instance of being is reached by reasoning from the observable
secondary instances, so the primary instance of moral goodness,
the *kalliston,* is inferred from the observable instances in
everyday conduct. Where they are good, it emerges as the best.

Through focal meaning, then, the nature of human happiness
will be found in contemplation only, while all other things that
are required by it or contribute towards it will come under its
range through their reference to it. These other things will not
add anything to its nature. If a non-Aristotelian example may
be permitted for the moment, the philosophical concept of God
as infinite being places in him the entire nature of existence.
Creatures bring more existents into the universe, but they do
not add anything to the nature of existence. With them there
are more beings but not more being in the world. Being in its
entirety remains located in the primary instance. In somewhat
parallel fashion for Aristotle the whole nature of happiness is
found in theoretical contemplation. Health, eduation, practical
virtue, mature life, social and political order, friendships,
sufficient wealth, amusements and leisure are all required to

make possible a life of this kind. Through focal meaning they come under it, without entering into its nature. They do not add more happiness to contemplation. Rather, they enable contemplation to be carried on, and in various ways have their focal reference to it. They are contained focally, not specifically, under its universal range.

The approach through focal reference does away with the stumbling block encountered by interpreters who make happiness a univocal notion and require that it be found as a nature in things other than contemplation. In the framework of focal meaning, happiness can for Aristotle consist essentially in contemplation alone, yet exclude nothing that is good or desirable for human beings. The life of practical virtue, that is, the life of social and political activity, is accordingly designated by the Stagirite as happiness in a secondary way (*deuterôs*—*E N*, 10.8,1178a9), for its purpose is to make the contemplative life possible for the citizens. All the other things follow in their various ways of focal reference. Bodily health, external goods, friendships, and amusements all play their part in the happiness of man insofar as they contribute to the free and abundant exercise of contemplation. In that way they are morally good and right. They are secondary instances of the *kalon*. They retain their own natures, but they are morally good through reference to the supreme instance of goodness. They are thereby included in human happiness. In particular, lively participation in Greek social and political life was explicitly designated as a secondary way of leading the good life, quite in accord with the tenet that a man can contemplate only in comparatively short intervals.

IV

With contemplation understood in this way as the nature of genuine human happiness, one may now ask what the contemplation is about, and where and when it takes place. What is contemplated in this vision is left vaguely described by Aristotle as the best and highest object. But what exactly is that object? Is it the activity of the mind itself, in the way an Aristotelian separate substance is eternal self-contemplation, leaving no room for the question "thought of thought of what?"[23] Or is the object the perfections of other separate substances? Or does it coincide with the object of metaphysics, the highest type of theoretical reasoning? Or is it the objects of the sciences and the fine arts, making the contemplation consist in what today would be called an intellectual or an esthetic life? Does the contemplation consist in intellectual life in general, by pursuing the various arts and sciences, and investigating their subject matter, with deep enjoyment in the attraction they offer?

These answers have been variously given by Aristotle's commentators. But no one of them is made explicit in the text of the Stagirite himself. He never seems to become specific on this issue. He is enthusiastic and waxes lyric in writing about the contemplative activity.[24] But nowhere does he say explicitly what the object contemplated is. He develops his reasoning as far as his principles allow. But he does not force them beyond their capacity. He feels no compulsion to systematize his thought into a rounded-out system. He is not afraid of having to leave loose ends. He remains in this regard a thoroughly honest thinker. His commentators down through the centuries have kept trying to bring the loose ends together. But in the present case they have had no decisive success within the Aristotelian context itself.

No matter how the object of supreme human happiness may be explained in this Aristotelian setting, it has to allow for significant discontinuity and plurality. A mind that is entirely incomposite and separate would enjoy the contemplation uninteruptedly throughout the whole of eternity. In contrast, human contemplation takes place on repeated occasions each in a definite time. It does not have its completion, its entire good, in any one of these passing acts of contemplation, but rather in a full lifetime. The reason is that a human person remains other than any individual acts of contemplation: ". . . human thought, or rather the thought of composite beings, is in a certain period of time (for it does not possess the good at this moment or at that, but its best, being something *different* from it, is attained only in a whole period of time)" (*Metaph.*, 12.9,1075a7–9; Oxford trans.).[25] Human beings are in the state of contemplation only at times, in contrast to eternal contemplation: "If, then, God is always in that good state in which we sometimes are, this compels our wonder; and if in a better this compels it still more" (7,1072b24–26; Oxford trans.).

The object of human contemplation, whatever it may be, is not, then, attained for Aristotle through continuous contemplation. Rather, it is achieved in discontinuous individual acts by individual human minds. Just as one swallow does not make a summer, a full lifetime of individual acts of contemplation is required for a person's happiness (*E N*, 1.7,1098a15–20). Moreover, though each individual perishes in death, the species goes on eternally.[26] In this perspective the supreme happiness of the individual and of the city-state coincide (2,1094b7–10). Quite as with Plato for whom virtue in the body politic was the same as virtue in the individual person yet could be seen written with larger letters in the functioning of the city-state, so for Aristotle (*E N*, 1.2,1094b7–10) the supreme human good appeared more divine and more perfect when viewed on the broader plane. Contemplation in each individual was looked upon as divine, but it was in the human race as a whole that this divinity was more evident and more striking.

The individual person, in fact, merged his own destiny in the destiny of the human species. It was his task to "start from what is good for each and make what is without qualification good good for each" (*Metaph.*, 7.3, 1029b6–7; Oxford trans. Cf. *E N*, 6.1, 1129b5–6). The way to this unqualified good was through the particular acts of the virtues, resulting in friendships and culminating in greatness of soul, the baffling virtue that "seems to be a sort of crown of the virtues; for it makes them greater, and it is not found without them" (*E N*, 4.3, 1124a1–3; Oxford trans.). The eternal contemplation in which the unqualified good consists is at the apex of an ordered universe (*Metaph.*, 12.10, 1075a16–25). From the immortal and divine duration "derive the being and life which other things, some more or less articulately but others feebly, enjoy" (*Cael.*, 1.9, 279a28–30; Oxford trans.).

The picture of human destiny becomes accordingly quite clear in its general outlines. It is inspired by a marvelous insight into the supreme worth of intellection just in itself. This supreme destiny was worked out by the human species in its individuals, primarily in the relatively few who were able to lead a life of theoretical contemplation, and secondarily in those who by their virtuous activity brought about the conditions in which that life was made possible. The people active in social and political life promoted the culture and the order that gave leisure for contemplation. Those engaged in the arts and crafts provided the sustenance as well as the material setting in which the contemplation could take place. They were all capable of happiness in a secondary way, because they shared in thought and virtue. On the other hand material goods and possessions, including animals and slaves, fulfilled the purpose of their existence by serving the needs of free men without sharing formally in happiness themselves.

This comprehensive understanding of human destiny centered decisively upon theoretical contemplation as the highest kind of thought. In that type of contemplation Aristotle saw sublime value. At times his glowing language might suggest some kind of a mystical intuition of its intrinsic worth. At least his lifelong engagement with it had left him enamored of its overwhelming beauty and its power to satisfy man's deepest yearnings. Considered as thoroughly divine in itself, it was what raised human life to the divine level and brought to full flower man's ultimate destiny.

From today's standpoints, however, the respect accorded human life in this Aristotelian view appears faulty. The interest focused upon operation rather than upon the human person. The few were favored rather than the many, for only a comparatively small number of people could attain *eudaimonia* in its primary instance. Weight was allowed to the reasoning that slavery can be natural because some human beings are meant by nature to be ruled by others and to work with their bodies rather than with their minds (*Pol.*, 1.5, 1254b19–34). Children could be considered to partake of happiness only on account of their promise of future activity (*E N*, 1.9, 1100a1–5). Deformed infants were to be "exposed," the euphemistic expression for being abandoned to die, with zero increase in population maintained by abortion in the very early stages of pregnancy (*Pol.*, 7.16, 1335b19–26). The respect for human life was sharply geared to ensuring conditions in which the comparatively few gifted individuals could engage in contemplation at intervals during their earthly existence.

V

These considerations, nevertheless, need not obscure the great merits in the Aristotelian conception of human destiny. The Stagirite's reasoning has brought to the fore, first of all, that one's destiny is a matter of individual choice. The choice is not haphazard. It calls for careful guidance by and intelligent submission to reason. Right reason shows that the morally good choice is the happiness that corresponds to man's nature and function as human.

Secondly, Aristotle has shown that human destiny consists essentially in theoretical contemplation. Here his basic instinct may be considered as sound, even though he fails to specify the object of the intellection. He sees the intellection, however, as eternal in the species only and not in each individual taken alone. In both the individual and the species he leaves it restricted to life on earth, carried on in the union of soul with body. The eternal thinking of the separate intellect without association with the perishable passive intellect can hardly be considered as *human* destiny.

Thirdly, Aristotle's explanation of knowledge as a union in which knower and thing known are identical in the actuality of cognition offers a way to establish theoretical contemplation as the possession of all goods whatsoever. It is the closest union possible. It is the most intimate way of possessing. As sketched by Aristotle, though, knowledge would seem to remain a way of being its objects in a secondary type of existence, in comparison to possession of them in their real external existence.

Fourthly and finally, the important Aristotelian doctrine of focal meaning runs through these considerations. It explains how moral reasoning can have a distinct type of truth, how *eudaimonia* can consist essentially in contemplation yet extend in its requirements to all other relevant goods, how intellection can have both active and passive principles, and how being in human cognition is a genuine though secondary way of existence.[27]

What will happen, then, when the wisdom of Aristotle is transposed into a Christian setting? Human destiny will indeed remain something chosen. But now, according to the revealed doctrine held by a Christian on religious faith, it has been chosen by a provident creator. Yet it will also be subject to the choice of the individual human person, who as a free agent now makes the correct choice not just on indications of nature alone but in conformity with nature habituated by grace. Man's ultimate destiny will still consist in intellection. But in the light of revealed doctrine the object of the intellection will be the triune substance of the divinity, in a beatific vision that will endure eternally in each individual soul. The destiny will in this way be supernatural, and the way to it will be through grace, prayer, and sacraments.

These are considerations accepted on religious faith. But as actually held religious beliefs they are phenomena that come thematically under the object of philosophy of religion. So viewed, they give rise to genuinely philosophical reflections and problems. Such problems are, for instance, how a person can freely choose his own destiny if it has already been divinely chosen for him, how habituation by grace may be brought under a category of being, how things can exist in the divine creative essence in a way far higher, far stronger, and far richer than the way they exist in themselves. Problems like these require discussion on the basis of strictly philosophical principles. Likewise philosophy has to determine continually its own competence and its own limits in regard to them. The Aristotelian philosophical framework will be surprisingly helpful, even though the overall picture of human destiny may be radically different in the Christian setting.

With the foregoing considerations about the philosophy of religion in mind, one may now go on to examine how the Aristotelian principles were applied brilliantly in Aquinas to the Christian conception of human destiny.

CHAPTER TWO

Human Destiny in Aquinas

I

Aristotelian philosophy had been influencing the structure of Christian thought in university circles for several decades before St. Thomas Aquinas began his career as teacher and writer. There need be little surprise that in commencing his *Summa contra gentiles* he should appeal to Aristotle's notion of wisdom and order. It is the function of wisdom to bring order into things, he recalls, according to one of the characteristics of a wise man that had been noted by the Stagirite.[1] Against that philosophical background the *Contra gentiles* was intended to be a summary of "the truth that the Catholic faith professes" (*CG*, 1.2, Assumpta).

The treatise begins with a look at the Aristotelian notions of order and orderly directing. Regulation of this kind, in Aquinas' interpretation, has to be taken from the goal intended. Going further in his own thinking, Aquinas adds that the ultimate purpose of a thing, no matter what it may be, is what its primary maker or movent intends. He applies this conclusion to the present problem: "But the primary originator and movent of the universe is intellect. Therefore the ultimate goal of the universe has to be the good proper to intellect."[2] Actual contemplation, the good that is characteristic of the intellect, is in this way presented as the supreme goal or purpose of the entire universe. It is presented, moreover, not just on the basis of something that follows from a thing's nature, as with Aristotle, but rather as something intended by the thing's primary efficient cause.

It is not hard, despite this difference, to see the Aristotelian structure in which Christian thought is here being developed. The ultimate purpose of the universe is located in intellection, quite in accord with the Aristotelian philosophical framework. But, Aquinas goes on, the good proper to the intellect is truth. Therefore truth has to be the ultimate purpose of the whole universe, not any truth at all but the truth that is the origin of all truth, the truth really identical with the primary source of existence for everything. The focal order of truth, so understood, corresponds exactly to the order of existence.[3] But the sense of the interpretation goes beyond anything in Aristotle.

In fact, a greatly enriched metaphysics can be seen back of this rapid reasoning. Forward reference is given (supra, n. 2) for the assertion that intellect is the "primary originator and movent of the universe." Aquinas himself (*CG*, 4.1, Competunt) claimed that the discussion in the first three books of the *Contra gentiles* is concerned with the way things divine are known through creatures by natural reason. This route is a metaphysics that proceeds from the existence of sensible things to subsistent existence. Subsistent being, so inferred, is infinite. It is not finite like the separate forms reached by the Aristotelian path of actuality and potentiality. In this the metaphysical reasoning of Aquinas is cogent, once its basis in the existence originally known through judgment is recognized.[4] However, in regard to the problem of human destiny it has a philosophically disconcerting effect. The infinite truth that is really identical with the infinite being of God is shown to be the supreme good sought by the human intellect. But as something infinite it is utterly unattainable for the merely natural capacity of an intellect that is finite, as in the case of man.

In the metaphysics of Aquinas, then, a gaping chasm of apparently infinite breadth looms up between human nature and its ultimate destiny. The human intellect has sufficient ability for reasoning to subsistent existence from the existence of sensible things.[5] But it is not proportioned to attaining subsistent existence as a nature and thereby having it as the object of its vision. It has no natural capacity for quidditative vision of infinite being. A created substance, Aquinas emphasizes, could reach such vision only through divine action.[6] Its attainment is something above the grasp of human power. In the first three books of the *Contra gentiles* Aquinas had given his answers to the first two questions that were later posed by Kant, about what can be known and about what should be done. The fourth and last book of that work leads up to what may serve as an answer for Kant's third question, the question of what a person may hope for. The book proposes to treat of doctrines that are above human reason, such as the Trinity and the Incarnation, and finally of "those things above reason that are awaited in the ultimate goal of men, such as the resurrection and glorification of bodies, the perpetual bliss of souls, and the things that are connected with these beliefs."[7] Because "above reason," these beliefs fit in with the metaphysical gap just noted.

The appalling prospect of an intellectual creature meant for knowing truth, yet without the natural capacity for quidditative knowledge of truth in its primary instance, is in this way faced by Aquinas. His recognition of and esteem for the intrinsic worth of intellection is no whit inferior to Aristotle's. He is accordingly repelled by the thought that an all-wise creative

providence would leave unbridged the intolerable chasm between an intellectual creature and its presumptive goal. He
writes in that vein at the beginning of the fourth book of the
Contra gentiles: "But since man's complete good consists in his
knowing God in full, lest so noble a creature should seem to be
altogether without purpose in the sense of not being able to
attain his proper goal, man is given a way by which he can
ascend into the cognition of God."[8]

This gratuitous way is different from the philosophical route
to God that has just been considered. It is a way by which
divine truth above the natural grasp of the human intellect
comes to men not through demonstration but through revelation. Only in the culmination after death will the human mind
be elevated to perfect intuition of what has been revealed.[9] The
fact that so exalted a destiny is the purpose for which man has
been created is in consequence not knowable through philosophic inquiry. Likewise the knowledge of the way towards it
through gratuitous means is outside the purview of philosophy.
Both are religious beliefs.

However, the new situation does prompt some philosophical
queries. For instance, there is the question whether human
nature just in itself should be regarded as "endless."[10] Was
Aristotle's failure to specify the object contemplated in human
eudaimonia a deficiency in his thinking, or did it represent faith-
fully the condition of human nature as known through philosophy? Certainly from the viewpoint of physical constituents man
could have been created without elevation to a supernatural
destiny. Certainly the fact of having a human form would give
him a purpose, as would follow on the ground of the Aristotelian relation of formal to final cause. Could man's destiny not
have been to reflect through the exercise of intellection and free
choice the perfections of his creator, thereby giving them external manifestation? Need a supernatural good be absolutely de-

manded, even though nature may remain open to it? A query like this is genuinely philosophical, despite the fact that it is asked in connection with a revealed doctrine.

Whatever way this openness of human nature to an end above itself may be expressed, it does explain the assertion of Duns Scotus that was made about a quarter of a century after the death of Aquinas. For Scotus the philosophers hold that nature is a completed whole, while the theologians know that it is deficient and requires supernatural completion through grace.[11] In the actual state of things, according to revealed doctrine, the creator chose first of all the purpose for which intellectual beings were to be made. It was for the beatific vision of the divine essence. Human nature accordingly was brought into existence endowed with an habituation of grace that equipped it for working towards its supernatural destiny. It never in actual fact had any other destiny. This was impervious to philosophical scrutiny. But for anyone who accepted it on supernatural faith it meant that the choice of one's supreme good was not to be made on the ground of what nature just in itself indicated, as with Aristotle, but on belief in the purpose the creator had in fashioning man, a purpose known through divine revelation. Human destiny becomes doubly a matter of choice, the choice of the sovereignly free creator in going above the exigencies of human nature, and the choice of the elevated human being in freely directing his life towards that ineffably sublime goal. The philosophical query reinforces the aspect of choice.

The first characteristic noted in the Aristotelian conception of human destiny remains therefore intact with Aquinas. Human destiny is something freely chosen, chosen now by God as well as by each individual person. But in the framework of the all-powerful and minutely efficacious providence on the part of a creator, a further philosophical query arises. How can the human choice be really free when it is produced in its entirety, down to its last detail, by the omnipotent and sovereignly free cause of all being? How are the two levels of freedom compatible with each other?

This is a difficulty Aristotle did not have to face. Lacking the conception of an infinitely powerful creator he could readily accept, in accord with the other main currents of Greek thought, the *fact* of human choice. He could find in it the distinguishing characteristic of practical philosophy. But Aquinas had to see human liberty in the setting of a supremely efficacious causality on the part of the first efficient cause of everything. He was well aware of the problem, and did not shy away from it in the least. His metaphysics of existence, however, did not present the long-drawn-out difficulties encountered by subsequent theologians, or by modern logicians in regard to Aristotle's sea-fight (*Int.*, 10,19a30). In the *Contra gentiles* (3.89, Item) he is content to recall the tenet that nothing can act in its own power without thereby acting in virtue of the divine power, with the result that God is the cause not only of the human will but also of its act of willing. In a later work he explains that the divine will, as primary cause, transcends the order of necessity and contingence. For effects it wishes to be necessary it assigns necessary causes, and for effects it wishes to be contingent it assigns contingent causes. But it itself is outside these differentiae, as "a cause that pours forth the whole of being and all its differentiae."[12]

Aquinas writes as though the human act of choosing freely is a highly refined instance of being, and issues precisely under that differentia from the primary cause of all being. There is no question here of the choice being predetermined by the primary cause. The determination is made by the secondary agent, the primary cause moving it to make the determination freely. This would be self-contradictory if the motion were being imparted by a finite cause, for the finitude would necessarily limit the motion, both specifically and existentially, to the one or to the other side of the proposed choice. But an infinite act of causing does not have that limitation. It is therefore efficacious in a way that leaves all options open to the secondary agent throughout the whole course of the motion. The human mind, able to comprehend only finite motions, tends to conceive the divine action moving the free agent on the model of the necessitating motion of a finite cause. Therapy is required to get rid of the limitation. The divine motion proceeds from subsistent existence, which has no limiting essence. The ease with which Aquinas handles the problem indicates that he is reasoning here as elsewhere against the background of a thoroughly existential metaphysics.

One might even go further and say that not only from the viewpoint of being but also from that of freedom does this explanation become imperative. The basic difficulty in accounting for the free act lies in its production of a definite effect while at the same time remaining open to producing something different or to not producing at all. The free act lacks the necessity that is intimately associated with the Aristotelian notion of being. In that perspective it appears incapable of theoretical explanation even though recognized as a fact. The difficulty faces anyone who tries to explain it ultimately through finite causes. Only when the basic or primary cause of the human free act, considered precisely from the angle of its freedom, is located in a cause of infinite efficacy can the freedom be accounted for. It is primarily caused by an agent that is undetermined by any limiting factor. The primary source and explanation of the creature's free act is thereby an efficient cause in no way determined to any definite physical effect. It is accordingly able to cause the free act without necessitating it. Under its causality all created choices remain free, including the choice of the beatific vision as one's ultimate happiness, one's destiny.

The gratuity of actual human destiny is a religious, not a philosophical, doctrine. But accepted as a belief, it comes thematically under the consideration of the philosophy of religion. The gratuitous character occasions the twofold philosophical query about the endlessness of nature just in itself and about the freedom of human choice under the infinitely efficacious choice on the part of a creator. Philosophical scrutiny of the belief shows that in it human destiny remains, as with Aristotle, something freely chosen by the individual person and something consisting essentially in intellection.

II

But while the object of the intellection was left unspecified in Aristotle, in Christian belief it is the triune God intuited face-to-face, in express contrast to knowledge had darkly through the mirror of creatures. At the beginning of the *Contra gentiles* (4.1, Ecce) the sublimity of this goal is driven home in a verse taken from the book of Job (26.14): "Who dares to contemplate the thunder of his full magnificence?" The mixing of the metaphors makes the impact all the more forceful. It stresses vividly the notion of intuiting, as opposed to believing. The staggering heights of this destiny above all natural human capacity are projected as though in a scene spread across a vast sky shattered by thunder and illumined by lightening flash. In the intuition "the divine majesty itself will be seen, and every perfection of things good."[13] Intense personal love follows (*ST*, 1–2.3.4).

With Aquinas, therefore, human destiny can no longer be regarded as just intellection without specification of the object contemplated. It is still the exercise of the highest human faculty upon its highest object. But the object of the contemplation is the divine substance. Though far above natural capacity, the way to it (supra, n. 8) is given by the supernatural providence of the creator who chose this goal for man. The basic orientation of man's substance towards it is conferred through the habitual grace that makes him partake of the divine nature and thereby become elevated to the level in which there is proportion to the face-to-face vision of God.[14] This way of sharing in the divine nature leaves human beings no longer just creatures of God. It makes them in reality his children, in the way St. Paul (Acts, 17.28) understood the Greek dictum "We are also his offspring." It was known through Christian faith.

Accepted as a religious belief, this habitual orientation towards the beatific vision could be discussed by Aquinas (CG, 4.59) in the Aristotelian philosophical setting of generation and corruption. It was a "spiritual generation," meant to be given the human soul through the sacrament of baptism. Where the sacrament cannot be received its effect may be supplied, likewise supernaturally and gratuitously, by its primary efficient cause (ST, 3.66.11). In fact, the condition mentioned by Aquinas, that a person's heart "be moved by the Holy Spirit to believe and to love God" (ibid.), would seem to be fulfilled by unbaptized persons who choose the morally good as best they know it rather than the morally evil: "After they have the use of reason, they are obliged to provide for their salvation. If they have done this, they will already be without original sin, grace intervening."[15] The new orientation pertains to the gratuitous. It is not *necessarily* limited to any particular sign or institution, but is subject to the first cause as to a free and intelligent agent. In the gratuitous order of the supernatural the relations of spiritual beings to their ultimate purpose need not be gauged on the model of necessitating natures. To the face-to-face character of the beatifying vision corresponds rather a person-to-person relationship in the dealings of the creator with his adopted children in the order of grace.

These tenets of the beatific vision as man's supreme destiny, and of the details of his journeying towards it, are matters of religious belief. Confronting philosophy of religion thematically, they give rise to important philosophical reflections. In Aristotle, human happiness had been assessed in terms of operation only. Unless a man engaged in intellection or in virtuous activity throughout a sufficiently long lifetime, he did not attain the destiny indicated by his nature. The dignity and worth of man was rated on his achievement here on earth. A child did not share in that happiness. Happiness was tarnished through serious misfortunes and sufferings. Happiness belonged to activity undertaken during natural life. In the Christian outlook of Aquinas, on the other hand, even infants were children of God through baptism and living members of his spiritual family. The attainment of salvation without any active contribution on the infant's part was made possible through the sacrament. Operation was no longer the one and only means on the part of the human person for reaching his ultimate goal.

From a philosophical viewpoint this shift of emphasis from operation to substantial orientation meant that one's own activity did not play the entire role in the attainment of human destiny. Room was left for sacraments (Aquinas, *CG,* 4.56, Nec) and for prayer.[16] Human personality, however, was by no means underplayed. Rather, it was elevated. For Aquinas (*ST,* 1.29.3, c) a person was "what is most perfect in the whole of nature." The subsisting in rational nature was the explanation given. Through grace the rational agent was raised to personal relationship with God during life on earth as son or daughter to father, instead of remaining in a vague general orientation to the highest object of his highest faculty. Oriented directly to God through habituation by grace, an intellectual creature possessed his worth and dignity even apart from the *activity* of thinking.

This different attitude may be seen indicated by the way Aquinas gauges the spontaneous respect for human life. While in Aristotelian fashion he accords (*ST,* 2–2.64.1, c) man full proprietary dominion over non-rational animals and the order of plant life, he reserves to God the dominion over human life (2–2.64.6.ad 5). After noting that suicide is against the natural inclination to live on, and is against the obligation of self-love, and also is as with Aristotle (*E N,* 5.11, 1038a9–14) against the good of the state, Aquinas adds as a fourth reason that life is a gift divinely bestowed on man, a gift remaining under the authority of God (*ST,* 2–2.64.5c). Insofar as a man through his free will is his own master he can licitly make his own disposi-tions in regard to leading this present life, which is regulated by his free choice. But departure from this life is not placed under man's free choice. It is subject to divine authority (ad 3). Kill-ing a human being directly is regarded by Aquinas as licit, nevertheless, when ordered by public authority for the common good, as in the punishment for crime or when necessary in the pursuit of criminals or in the defense of the country against enemy soldiers. Otherwise it may be intended only indirectly in self-defense (2–2, 64.7, c). An immediate personal relationship of man to God may be readily seen underlying this respect for human life, as based upon a divine dominion over it that is not waived by the creator in the case of private individuals but only in the case of public authority where required by the common good.[17] On account of this immediate relationship a man does not own his or any other person's life in the sense of having the right to do away with it at will.

III

The foregoing considerations indicate how deeply the specification of the object contemplated in supreme human hap-

piness can influence life on earth. Aquinas has no illusion whatever about the nature of the Aristotelian contemplation. It is a
happiness enjoyed in temporal life, an imperfect happiness. It is
the happiness of a way *(via)* towards the supernatural contemplation of the divine essence through unmediated vision. This
destiny is the perfect contemplation of God, a tenet that on
earth can only be believed in through faith. To it is oriented all
philosophical cognition of God, imperfect cognition based upon
what is known through creatures.[18]

The language of the relation of imperfect to perfect, and of
orientation towards the perfect instance, brings up at once the
Aristotelian viewpoint of focal meaning. The good life here
upon earth, the fullness of intellection in the present terrestrial
state, Aquinas is implying, gets its meaning as happiness from
the supernatural destiny to which it is related through divine
providence. It is a happiness through being a way to that supreme destiny. It has to be proportioned to that goal not
through naturally knowable means but by means known
through divine enlightenment.[19] This orientation, as already
noted in the preceding section, is a result of the grace conferred
basically through the sacraments. Instead of the Aristotelian
habituation through just the natural virtues, the habituation
through grace directs the whole temporal life of man towards
the beatific contemplation of the divine essence. Life on earth is
in this way assumed into human destiny, as the journey towards
it, and as the object that gives it its meaning. As with Aristotle,
however, the details of the practice of the virtues in daily living
are to be regulated on each occasion by right reason.[20]

Yet focal reference of all human activity towards the supernatural happiness of the beatific vision cannot help but work
profoundly upon the functioning of right reason in a person's
everyday life. Reference to the supreme instance of goodness is
what gives the secondary instances their specification as good.

For Aristotle the highest instance of moral goodness, the *kalliston,* was located in theoretical contemplation. Through relation to it all other things were morally good, *kala.* Moral goodness was first recognized by men in its secondary instances, human actions, in accord with their conformity to correct moral habituation. The immediately experienced moral goodness was explained philosophically through its highest naturally knowable instance, intellectual contemplation. But through Christian faith the object of that highest instance becomes specified. The *kalliston* becomes the face-to-face vision of the divine essence. It is in relation to a supernatural primary instance, then, that all other instances have their moral goodness. The morally good becomes absorbed and sublated in the sacred, or the holy, or the saintly, as expressed in religious language.

True, people who are not enlightened by Christian faith may neglect or expressly reject this explanation of what they spontaneously assess as moral goodness. Philosophically they may still invoke goodness in general as their norm, without specifying it to the sacred or the holy. They may even feel some revulsion at characterizing ordinary good actions as saintly or holy or sacred. Yet for Aquinas (see supra, n. 15) any person who has the use of moral reason is either habituated towards his supernatural end by grace, or is turned away from it. There is no neutral state of nature, in reality. The person who judges an action to be morally good is making the judgment, though without explicitly knowing it, on the basis of his orientation through grace towards the beatific vision, the actual and factual *kalliston.*

The understanding of moral goodness through focal reference to a specified primary instance will therefore have deep influence on human conduct. It allows all everyday activities to be looked upon as means of sanctification and as supernaturally meritorious. It gives the dimension of the sacred and the holy to all human life. In certain instances it may require moral decisions that run counter to what could be philosophically justified on the basis of merely natural morality. On merely natural grounds the attitude extolled in the Christian martyrs in acceptance of death rather than the burning of a bit of incense on a pagan altar might be hard to justify. Unless specific knowledge of one true God as opposed to false gods is admitted, the moral propriety of witnessing with one's life to the one in preference to the others might well be questioned. Early Christians were in fact judicially charged with atheism. The acceptance of a monastic vocation, the practice of what Hume called "the whole train of monkish virtues,"[21] the obligation of priestly celibacy, and questions concerned with the sanctity of human life and its procreation, may be assessed quite differently when the norm of morality is supernatural. Right reason now functions on a new ground.

These are just illustrations of the way the dimension of the holy or the sacred penetrates human conduct when the supreme instance of moral goodness is located in the beatific vision as the specified and supernatural object of contemplation. Through focal meaning man's life upon earth is incorporated into his supernatural destiny, as the preparation for or way *(via)* towards it. Aquinas's explanation of intellectual activity here on earth as imperfect happiness oriented towards the perfect, places the assessing and discussion of it, quite obviously, in the framework of Aristotelian focal meaning. The sacred, as accepted on religious faith, is thematically open to his study in this philosophical setting.

IV

Besides allowing for a supernatural destiny freely chosen for man by his first efficient cause, the existential outlook of

Aquinas adds two further considerations of importance towards a philosophical understanding of human destiny. One bears on the different ways in which a thing can exist in intellection. The other concerns the existence of the spiritual soul, an existence given through creation and therefore not dependent on bodily union for its endurance.

For Aquinas a thing can have three ways of existing. Its first and most fundamental way of existence is in the divine intellect. There it is the same in reality as the divine essence, differing only in concept. The second way is by existing in itself, or in an angelic mind. Both these types of existence depend immediately upon the first type. The third way of existing is in the human intellect, and is based immediately upon the existence of the things in themselves.[22]

The existence of things in the divine intellect is accordingly for Aquinas a much stronger and more perfect existence than their existence in themselves. It is prior to the real existence in the created world, and not dependent on it. It is an existence that lasts forever, because it is really identical with the creative essence.[23] This eternal existence of things may be found instinctively surmised at times. On the death of a family pet dog known from their earliest conscious years, children will react with the spontaneous conviction that some day they will be with Heidi again. Browning was able to write in his poem "Abt Vogler" (1.69): "There never shall be one lost good; what was, shall be as before." Both the instinctive reaction and the poetic inspiration seem well grounded in reality when they are assessed from the viewpoints of Aquinas' metaphysics. In its highest point of elevation the existence of every creature is eternal. To the child one has of course to explain that the dog will never exist again in itself, that is, in the way he has learned that the human soul continues to exist after bodily death. The perpetual existence of the soul in itself is a theme crucially relevant to the problem of human destiny, and still remains for close philosophical consideration. But for the moment the point is that all things whatsoever have eternal existence in the divine creative intellect, and that this is the highest type of existence they can have.

All things, it will mean, are possessed in the beatific vision of the divine creative essence. They are possessed cognitionally in it in their highest kind of existence. Anything missed or sacrificed for the sake of the right or the holy is accordingly never lost. Rather, eternal possession of it is assured. "Possession," in fact, may be a weak word here. The "possession" consists in being those things cognitionally, and not in the comparatively weak way of a cognition that follows upon and is dependent upon the things in their sensible existence. Rather, it is like the angelic cognition in having them as objects in their highest way of being. In the gradated orders of existence listed by Aquinas (supra, n. 22) the existence of things in the divine intellect is prior to their existence in themselves, while their existence in themselves is prior to their existence in present human cognition. It is not hard to see in this perspective the definitive answer to the objection that contemplation is a shadowy and unreal possession of things, like having them in a day dream. On the contrary, just as existence for sensible things in themselves is real in comparison with their cognitional existence in the human mind at present, so their existence in the beatific cognition is of a higher type than their real existence just in themselves. It is in this sense that "every perfection of things good" (supra, n. 13) is attained in the beatific contemplation, when explained in the metaphysical perspective of Aquinas.

From one important angle, however, existence in one's self looms uppermost. It is in one's own self that human destiny is worked out and achieved. Though ineffably high, the beatific vision is cognitional. The soul enjoying it becomes and is the objects by way of cognitional existence, not by way of real existence. The soul remains a really different being from God and from all other things, despite the closest and most exalted union in the cognitional existence. There is no thought of pantheism here. Even in saying that God is the existence of all things, Aquinas carefully explains that God is their existence not formally but by way of efficient and exemplar causality.[24] In real existence they remain really distinct. For Aquinas it is in one's own really distinct existence, and not in the thinking of any separate intelligence, that the supreme contemplation, in which "the actuality of mind is life," is attained by each individual. Aristotle's phrasing continues to be apt, but it now characterizes a life experienced by the individual human soul as agent.

For Aristotle the distinctive intellectual life of the individual, as differentiated through the forms received from sensible things immaterially and made intelligible by the agent intellect, came to an end in bodily death. There was no memory remaining to constitute a distinct personality.[25] This was in accord with the Aristotelian philosophy of nature, in which (*De an.*, 1.4,408b1–31) the individual man, the composite of matter and form, was the cognitive agent with the soul functioning as instrument. As usual, Aristotle was careful not to go further than his premises allowed. He made no explicit denial of the soul's immortality. But his thought did not develop an explicit affirmation of its continued existence after bodily death.

In Aquinas, on the other hand, the Aristotelian argument (*De an.*, 3.4,429a10–b22) that human thinking transcends material limitations is developed in an existential framework. With him the argument shows that the individual agent whose thought is not restricted to the material order has also an existence that transcends its material setting. In consequence the soul, not the composite, is the immediate subject of existence. As the formal cause of its own existence, the human soul can no more be separated from its existence than from itself. Aquinas does not push the cogency of this reasoning any further than his own philosophical premises allow. He concludes to the indestructibility of the spiritual soul, rather than to its immortality in the sense of life after bodily death. But, quite rightly, he takes for granted that an indestructible soul will readily be accepted as an immortal soul.[26]

For the purposes of the present problem, then, Aquinas' cogent demonstration of the indestructibility of the human soul provides the required metaphysical underpinning for a contemplation that lasts perpetually in the individual human being. Instead of intellection continued successively in individuals, though eternally in the human species, the location of supreme happiness is now in the perpetual contemplation exercised by each individual soul.

V

In Aquinas, then, the philosophical account of human destiny is developed against an easily recognized Aristotelian background. Supreme human happiness consists in intellection. But it is now intellection with a definitely presented object, an object accepted on religious faith. Further, it is a contemplation that will continue perpetually in every individual who has once attained it in its highest instance. It is also something that has been freely chosen for human beings by their first efficient cause. But it is still something to be chosen freely and pursued freely by each human being, the creator fashioning free causes to serve him freely as he fashioned necessary causes in the lower orders of things to serve him necessarily.

The different type of metaphysics that enabled Aquinas to use the Aristotelian concepts in his own presentation of what his faith taught on human destiny deserves careful consideration. His insight regarding existence as the actuality of all actualities allowed him to reason cogently to a God whose nature is existence and whose proper effect is existence. This meant that all else received existence from him first through creation, and then, in generation and accidental change, through his concurrence, existence that was maintained through his conservation.[27] Each spiritual soul, moreover, received existence directly through creation. This metaphysics served as a marvelously appropriate underpinning for the now person-to-person relationship between each human individual and his maker, which allowed human destiny to be gauged in the context of personality rather than just of nature. On the natural plane this was in full accord with the Scriptural (Acts, 17.28) adage that "in him we live and move and have our being." Life remained thoroughly God-centered.

At the same time human destiny took on the aspect of focal meaning that pervaded the Aristotelian metaphysics. The imperfect found its meaning in the perfect primary instance. So, for Aquinas, the Aristotelian perfect happiness became only a stage, something imperfect as a way to the perfect happiness of the beatific vision.[28] In this setting human destiny is something imperfectly achieved on earth, and perfectly only after bodily death. The worth these considerations have for human destiny today will play an important role in the topic of the next and concluding chapter.

CHAPTER THREE

Human Destiny in the Contemporary World

I

No less than in the case of St. Thomas Aquinas, the problems of human destiny today have to be faced by a Catholic thinker in the context of his religious faith. The same basic beliefs that were at work in the great thirteenth-century master will continue to act as the beacon. Human destiny will still be kept on the supernatural level. It will be something above the unaided natural powers of man to know or to attain. Life on earth will be viewed as a way, a *via,* to the beatific vision of the divine essence. Happiness on earth, this means, will be regarded as a preparatory stage. Present life is accordingly, just as with Aquinas, accepted as part of human destiny. But it is a part that is imperfect, and that gets its meaning as destiny from a perfect instance beyond the ken of merely natural human reason.[1]

These are religious beliefs. They are not philosophical principles or conclusions. Yet thematically for the philosophy of religion they now raise problems much more complicated than those of the thirteenth century, at least in regard to destiny on earth. As Aristotle repeatedly noted, man is by nature a political or social animal.[2] In this respect genuinely philosophical problems need to be encountered today in an attitude considerably different from the mentality that prevailed in the Middle Ages. They require sensitive consideration against the changed background of social and political conditions. They must likewise be thought out in the light of the vast expansion of human knowledge that has taken place in the last seven centuries. Intensely personal though human destiny may be, it has to be achieved on earth in active solidarity with contemporary ways of thinking. Here delicate issues arise for Catholic philosophy.

The Catholic thinker today no longer faces an area of limited horizons within which only three religious laws prevailed, the Jewish, the Christian and the Islamic. Rather, he is confronted by a civilized world in which those three traditions are professed by perhaps somewhat less than half of mankind, even when the three are taken together. All three had shared in common the belief in a unique and provident God, the belief in man's ultimate destiny in a life after bodily death, and the belief in each person's accountability to a supreme judge after death for all deeds during bodily life. There had been deviations, and underground survivals of pagan thought. But these were relatively minor, or were considered heretical. The land of Prester John and the kingdoms that came to be sketched in Marco Polo were vague and too marginal to enter into the main discussion. For practical purposes the dialogue was limited to traditions that believed in God and in a prophetic revelation of the divine will, as well as in the providence of the creator in regard to his creatures on earth.

Today these Scriptural beliefs can no longer be looked upon globally as dominant. In particular, the Catholic belief in its fullness is limited to profession by only a minority, perhaps not exceeding seven hundred million persons out of a global population of over four billion. Non-Catholic Christians have become formally separated from the Catholic ecclesial structure. They share in various degrees in its tenets while rejecting some or many of them definitively. Differences, moreover, have become wide-ranging among those who are nominally Christians, approaching in some cases the point where beliefs diverge hardly if at all from naturally knowable truth. In this latter extreme the supernatural is either expressly or effectively denied.

At the same time there is no shadow of doubt regarding a deep and active spirit of religious faith to be found in non-Catholic Christians and in the adherents of Jewish and Muslim beliefs. Likewise people who live according to the teachings of Buddhism and Hinduism and other traditional religions manifest profound and genuine spiritual orientation. Also persons who profess no religious beliefs at all, or are at the most deistic or humanistic in their outlook, may maintain wholesome moral standards in their daily living. All this becomes evident to today's Catholic upon closer association in actual life. Much to admire is brought to light in people of all these convictions upon sufficient acquaintance with them. The notion that they are cut off from true human destiny here on earth is instinctively repellent. They cannot be dismissed lightly today with the acrimonious labels of schismatics, heretics, or pagans. Ecumenical writers, in fact, go very far in emphasizing the good to be found in other beliefs or ways of life, and at times may seem to water down substantially the content of Catholic doctrine in order to bring it more in line with generally accepted notions.

On the other hand, large and organized segments of humanity vehemently attack belief in God. They combat all religion, and explicitly aim to suppress it. With them it is no longer a question of difference in religious belief, but a campaign to eliminate the belief entirely. How are people of this orientation to be regarded as participants in true human destiny here on earth, namely as children of God and as enemies to be forgiven? They seem much further removed, obviously, from the fullness of divine revelation than are the well-meaning persons who differ upon particular religious doctrines. They seem to verge on the point of rendering the problem of coexistence philosophically insoluble, because of their studied and open hostility.

At any rate, the panorama shows that the greater portion of mankind today does not share the Catholic's view of human destiny. Even with those who hold that it consists in the Trinity seen face-to-face, there are sharp differences about the way of journeying to it in life upon earth. These differences upon human destiny during its present imperfect stage often are of primary importance for practical life. They give rise to sharp conflicts regarding divine worship, respect for the sacredness of human life, and problems of marriage, sexual morality, public education, and other matters of common concern. Yet Catholics breathe the same social, commercial, and geopolitical air as everybody else. They share a common world with the others. Telecommunications and highly sophisticated media bring all the peoples of the earth into close union. The liaison is instant. All human life is now to be led in McLuhan's one global village. How can it be carried on harmoniously when views on its purpose differ in so fundamental a fashion?

Obviously there are questions for philosophy here. To what extent are the various views irreconcilable? To what extent have they elements in common? How can the common be used as the basis for cooperative undertakings, without jeopardy to the essentials of what each party claims it cannot give up? These are questions that have often to be ironed out on a rational level. Even though a precise concept of human destiny is held on religious faith, the ways in which its consequences are to be put into practice is as in other practical areas a matter for right reason. Regardless of how personal a legislator may be, he does not, as Plato (*Plt.*, 295AB) so aptly highlighted, sit at every-one's side to dictate in detail the right course of action. Deliberation and rational choice are the prerogative of human freedom. How, then, are the differences to be met?

II

In the question on the way clashing concepts of human destiny may function in a common social and political world, the first important consideration emerges lucidly from what has already been seen in Aristotle and Aquinas. Human destiny is something that is freely chosen. It is freely chosen, moreover, by the individual person and not directly by the community. Aristotle recognized in the same Greek community the different choices in different individuals. Some chose sensual pleasure, others chose fame and prestige and power, still others claimed to choose money-making or goodness in general. There were further views too numerous and too superficial to be mentioned by him in detail. Though the Stagirite urged legislators to provide the framework for the education and social environment that would habituate the citizens to make the right choice in regard to a *eudaimonia,* he showed no signs of wanting to impose from on high on any individual the life of theoretical contemplation. The thorough training in virtues from earliest years can hardly be looked upon in any other light than as an acknowledgment that the pursuit of the contemplative life depends on the individual's choice. Correspondingly for Aquinas the creator fashioned free agents to serve him freely. God wished them to accept freely the supernatural goal for which he had destined them. Likewise each act of working towards it during the imperfect happiness here on earth had to be free in order to be meritorious for that ultimate goal. For both these thinkers the destiny of each individual was something to be chosen freely by the individual himself. With Aristotle the true destiny was indicated clearly enough by man's nature. With Aquinas it was gratuitously chosen by God. But with both there was moral obligation to make the correct choice, and to be moral the decision had to be free.

From the eighteenth century on this prerogative of choosing one's own individual pursuit of happiness has been called an inalienable human right. The notion of what is owing to someone through the virtue of justice is of course prominent in Aristotle. Likewise in Aquinas the term *jus,* which Neoscholastic writers have unhesitatingly used for the modern notion of a right, retains the objective sense of what is owing to a person in justice. But the notion of a right as something possessed by a person, something in the individual, is a modern development. With the prerogative of free will goes the responsibility of providing for oneself in regard to both choice of ultimate destiny and use of the means necessary to attain it. Hence the unhindered choice of destiny and access to the means to work it out in practical life are owing to the individual person in justice. So, conversely, the individual may be regarded as having a right to them. Basically the rights will extend to nourishment, sustinence, education and income, and to opportunities for friendships, association, and whatever else is necessary for leading the good life on earth as a way *(via)* to the ultimate goal.

Here firm regulation becomes necessary. Appropriate distribution of goods, if they are to serve their purpose adequately, is imperative. Defense against aggressors is required. Positive communal arrangements are needed to provide and increase opportunity for all, especially for the handicapped and underprivileged. Public authority has to be set up to assure these conditions. It has to be given the means of coercion, physical where warranted. But in this regard deep conflict can arise. Aristotle, in a spirit of Greek moral optimism, seemed to take for granted that right reason on both sides would settle the differences. Yet in actual practice reason in the ruler and reason in the subject come at times to opposite conclusions on particular items. In the Middle Ages individuals and associations asserted their liberties or privileges ("private laws") against the dominating public authority. Feudal lords had their own proper authority in matters in which the overlord was not to interfere. Cities proclaimed their freedoms vis-à-vis the king's domination. The *Magna Charta* guaranteed the liberty of the church in what were recognized as things spiritual and to individuals a trial by their peers instead of judgment solely from the side of the ruler. Privileges and liberties of this kind, against the coercive authority, were what later came under the label of "rights" in the various bills of rights, such as the French "Declaration of the Rights of Man and Citizen" (1791), the "International Declaration of the Rights of Man" (1929), the "American Declaration of the Rights and Duties of Man" (Bogotá, 1948), and the "Universal Declaration of Human Rights" (United Nations, 1948).[3]

When the notion "right" was specified in this sense in the seventeenth century it still retained connection with right reason. It was meant to signify the liberty to use according to right reason one's natural faculties.[4] It was based on right reason vis-à-vis unjust use or failure of public authority, or unjust aggression by others. It allowed right reason in the individual person an innate respect of its own, something much more in accord with the dignity of the human person than a requirement that he understand himself to be wrong if his judgment goes against that of the community, or the penalty that he be sublated or liquidated into an ongoing dialectical flow.[5] In a word, it recognized in the ordinary good citizen the ability to see what is morally right in cases where authority tends to be negligent or tyrannical, or where common custom has degenerated into abuse. The reasoning of those in authority need not always be right reason. It may require balancing through the weight of reasoning done by others.

Recognition of the individual citizen's liberty to choose his or her ultimate destiny is inherent in today's liberal democracies. The individual is no longer required to meld personality into a proclaimed national mission. "We preach no manifest destiny"[6] sums up this attitude quite aptly. The attitude is implicit in guarantees of religious freedom; for religion, if it is to have any real meaning, has to have man's supreme destiny as its concern. The Christian location of that destiny in a supernatural life can account for the factual unwillingness of a liberal democracy to come to grips with the question. A liberal democracy is ready to leave the problem to the individuals or to churches because, quite rightly, it can see no manifest answer. In ancient Athens Plato (*Apol.,* 21A–22A) had Socrates make the rounds of outstanding people in public life, interviewing them and questioning them one by one on the *kalon kagathon,* the properly human good. Even though they were reputed to be wise, Socrates found that they did not know anything about it. He concluded that he was wiser than they, because he at least knew that he did not know anything about so lofty a topic. They did not even know that!

Like Socrates, then, the present-day liberal democracy exercises wisdom in disclaiming to know anything about man's ultimate destiny. In consequence, it does not want to interfere with the individual's religious choice. It continually experiences secondary instances of the moral good in everyday living. From them it is able to draw the broad principles upon which it regulates the common life of the state. It allows its courts to make the particular decisions required for the enforcement of its laws. But it does all this in a way that permits the individual persons to exercise their liberties and work out their supreme

destiny as they see fit. Wherever on the other hand a dictatorship or an ideology prescribes a natural destiny for its citizens,
the individual person can only struggle and fight for his rights
as best he can, waiting till the relentless course of history proves
to be the nemesis of wrongly conceived goals.

This situation, however, raises important problems for
Catholic philosophy, concerning education, marriage, and freedom of expression. Thematically the philosophy of religion faces
the question of rights that proceed from the liberty to choose
the supernatural destiny. Aristotle had shown that training in
virtues from earliest years is required for correct choice of
eudaimonia. Christian belief adds the requirement of habituation
through grace by means of baptism and the other sacraments,
and by a life of prayer. In that regard it belongs to the parents to
bring to maturity as best they can, in both the natural and
supernatural orders, the life they have procreated. Only when
their offspring has reached the stage of making decisions in full
rationality is their responsibility terminated. This is not an
interference with the liberty of the children. Rather, it is the
preparation for the exercise of that liberty. The suggestion of
letting a child wait till maturity to make the decision about
whether he should be baptized and what religion he should
embrace, is as unfounded as would be the project of leaving his
maternal language and his culture to the time when he can
make his own reasoned choice. To be able to make his choices
morally, the correct habituation under others has to precede.
Once freedom of choice for supernatural destiny is recognized by
the state, the consequent religious rights of individuals in regard to marriage and to education of children follow in
philosophical sequence.

Correspondingly the church, which unlike the liberal democracy does have in the Christian conception the obligation of
preaching man's destiny, can claim under the title of liberty of

expression or free speech the right to exercise this competence. Coercion of an adult to receive baptism against his will, or appeal to a temporal sword to enforce the choice of the destiny proclaimed through preaching, is on grounds of innate human liberty incompatible with this mission. Basic and inviolable is the tenet that human destiny must remain something freely chosen. The obligation to choose it correctly is moral, not coercive.

III

With this freedom of choice duly and unhesitatingly granted in regard to human destiny, however, some further philosophical problems arise for anyone who believes that all men without exception are meant by their creator for the beatific vision of the Trinity, and that the teaching of the way to this destiny has been confided to a definite church. Are all those who in good conscience cannot see their way to accept this supernatural goal, or who are unable in good faith to accept in detail the path towards it that has been thus proclaimed, cut off from all access to it? If they are not so cut off, in what manner do they enjoy orientation towards it? How can their ultimate destiny be at all the same as with those who work towards the beatific vision in the way of a definite religion? How can their life on earth, with outlooks so different, be in reality a journey towards the one ultimate goal chosen for them by their divine maker?

What is basically involved in this problem is the aspect of the sacred or the holy. Its primary instance is the divine nature. A creator known through the philosophical way of existence, as with Aquinas, is infinite in perfection. So reached, the divine nature infinitely surpasses finite human apprehension. It has depths that unaided human reason cannot hope to fathom. Yet through grace and revelation it is known as triune, and under this aspect it is the object of the beatific vision, in which according to Christian revelation the ultimate destiny of man has been placed by the creator.

Under that supernaturally knowable aspect the divine nature may be regarded as the primary instance of the sacred or the holy, when looked at from the philosophical viewpoint of focal meaning. It is as such proclaimed to be unique in the wording of the doxology, "For you alone are holy."[7] The other instances of the sacred can be so only by focal reference, as in the case of saintly persons, holy places, sacred objects. The full nature of the sacred, therefore, can according to Christian revelation be found only in the Trinity. People are holy only because they share in secondary fashion the divine nature, through grace. Actions are holy only because they tend towards the Trinity as the ultimate destiny of men. Church buildings are sacred because dedicated to divine worship. Cemeteries are sacred because they contain the mortal remains of persons whose lives were directed towards the beatific vision. Focal reference towards the Trinity pervades all these religious applications of the notion of sacred or holy or numinous.

From this philosophic consideration emerges the conclusion that the norm for judging the sacred does not lie in a common notion univocally abstracted from all its instances, in the way the notion of a man may be abstracted equally well from Plato or Aristotle or any other individual man. Rather, as in the case of health or of being, the aspect is found as a nature in a primary instance only. When found elsewhere, it is shared focally in various degrees and relationships by things really other than itself. It does not manifest itself as a common denominator that applies in its fullness to even the least of its participants. Quite to the contrary, it occurs in its full meaning in the primary instance alone. The primary instance is accordingly its measure.

Understood in this focal manner, then, the same object is

seen throughout all the instances of the sacred, in spite of the varying degrees. It is seen in the conduct of believers in the Trinity, who strive towards their supernatural goal in all their ordinary activities as well as in their prayer and sacramental life. It is likewise seen by the Christian in the lives of those who without belief in the Trinity or the sacraments aim to love and serve their creator throughout their earthly existence. It is also seen by him in deists, humanists, atheists, and others who with high moral standards pursue the good that is apparent in the world around them. From the Christian viewpoint these are all oriented, though without explicit awareness of it, towards the beatific vision. All the good actions are prompted by divine grace. Under present providence there is no neutral state of nature, and consequently no good work that does not have intrinsic orientation towards the Trinity. There is no other supremely final goal. What all these persons are unknowingly seeking, and working towards in all the good they do, is the beatific vision and the way to it through Christ. In this spirit the prayer in the Advent liturgy is addressed to Christ: "Come to meet those who, although they do not know it, are expecting you."[8] The goal they are really seeking is perfect beatitude, which can be had only after death, and on earth the way to it, which is through Christ. That is the Christian belief.

For the Christian, accordingly, the whole moral order becomes sublated into the realm of the sacred. Just as the lower orders of creation are oriented towards serving man, so every human being is in fact destined for the unmediated vision of the Trinity, and in consequence is provided with the grace that raises him or her to the supernatural level of life, either through baptism or through a voluntary turning towards the good in actual conduct. In this vein the fourth Gospel does not hesitate to speak in its opening lines of the divine Word that "enlightens every man," and other Scriptural passages can insist on the necessity of divine help for doing anything good.[9] As on the level attainable by philosophy no action can be performed without the divine premotion and concurrence, so on the supernatural level under present providence no good can be done apart from the promptings of divine grace. The aspect of the sacred runs in consequence through all human conduct, regardless of knowledge or ignorance of it on the part of the agent.

It is the aspect of grace, then, that in the perspective of Christian revelation demands respect for every human being. Under present providence all are members of the same supernatural family. The sublime truth that we are also God's offspring could be recognized through affectivity by the Greek poets. Their poetic intuition could be taken up by St. Paul (Acts, 17.28) and justified through Christian revelation. The supernatural habituation flows out into all their good actions. The one and the same aspect of the sacred furnishes amply sufficient ground for respecting the basic goodness in the aims and actions of every well-intentioned person, regardless of differences in religious beliefs or in cultural or political tendencies. That aspect of the sacred is there to serve as the fundamental consideration in the dealings of human beings with one another. Considered theoretically, the firm and enduring basis for ecumenism and for worldwide cooperation with all mankind is patently present in the notion of human destiny that is proposed by Christian faith. The foundation is vividly there. With goodwill present on all sides, one is not facing the mentality of culpable unbelief and schism and heresy against which the Scriptures thunder. The fullness of revealed truth is not, in this perspective, to be diminished or watered down in its primary instance. Nevertheless the truth must be respected in all its other instances without exception. In this way the full sublimity of the truth itself, and not a univocally common denominator, remains the measure.

IV

Viewed theoretically, therefore, the aspect of the sacred might be expected to ensure harmonious and urbane interchange of views whenever discussions about religious beliefs arise. Present everywhere, it should prompt courteous, friendly, and inspiring dialogue. The results envisaged would be mutual help and encouragment. Actual experience, nevertheless, often paints the picture in quite different colors. When a religious topic is introduced, tempers may rise and voices get strident. Repeatedly history narrates tales of bitterness and even extreme cruelty when clashes over the sacred have occurred. Today valiant and persevering efforts towards ecumenism and universal goodwill keep encountering difficulties and stumbling blocks that augur a long difficult road ahead. Mutual understanding and appreciation in setting the tone, though professedly desired by all, in reality seem yet a long way off. Especially, the prospect of organic Christian unity lies beyond the foreseeable future. Shattered for centuries, it may still need centuries for restoration. There is no room for being naïve.

What causes so much trouble? Theology may see at work preternatural forces with which philosophy has no means of grappling.[10] But there are some important aspects of these religious phenomena that can be discussed with profit on the philosophical level. One of them is basic for dialogue between believers and nonbelievers. It concerns the legitimacy of admitting even for purposes of discussion the possible openness of human reason to the embracing of truths that cannot be attained through its own natural powers. Here philosophy has its role to play. In showing that man and the universe are the creation of an infinitely powerful and intelligent God, philosophical reasoning can do much to assuage the indignant surge of inborn pride that wells up at the suggestion of truths that are in principle beyond the power of unaided human reason to attain. Philosophical investigation can probe the nature of the human faculties and show how their range is confined in each case to what their objects allow. Their immediate objects, upon which all human conclusions depend, are the limited things of the sensible world. Their scope, accordingly, is always limited. In contrast, reason can demonstrate that the nature of God is existence, something that in its own nature is unlimited in respect of every perfection. No ground can be made apparent, then, why there may not be truths beyond the natural reach of the human mind, truths that may be revealed to man out of the infinite knowledge of God. Establishing the *fact* of divine revelation is, of course, a different matter. But the possibility of openness in the human intellect to truths coming from divine revelation is enough to allow dialogue between believer and nonbeliever. The legitimacy of communication and genuine discussion between them can in this way be presented and upheld by philosophical considerations. Each can listen to the other.

On the side of the nonbeliever, the quite obvious limitations of human intelligence, as they are made manifest by philosophy, can show rationally enough that there is possibly room for divinely revealed truths. At least, the topic merits discussion. Under philosophic scrutiny human reason refuses to crown itself as a goddess in the spirit of the French revolution at Paris. Modesty in regard to its natural capacities ceases to appear hollow or obsequious. The possibility that there are more things in heaven and earth than can be dreamt of in one's philosophy is shown by philosophy itself. Intelligence and rationality no longer appear as a monopoly of the nonbeliever. He recognizes them in his opponent, paving the way for dialogue. A bit of quiet philosophical reflection should reveal the openness from his side.

On the side of the believer, philosophy shows correspondingly that sensitivity to the feelings and the disposition of his opponent is in order. Accusations of obtuseness or lack of good-will in refusing to accept the cogency of theistic arguments fall wide of the mark. In point of fact, philosophy is pluralistic. From the starting points of some philosophies the existence of God does not follow. If their first principle is that being is necessarily material, as in standard materialisms, the existence of a totally immaterial being is excluded. If, as with Kant (*KRV*, B595–730), human concepts are meant for application only in the world of possible experience, they cannot lead to anything outside that order, and in consequence cannot be used by theoretical reason to prove the existence of a transcendent god. If human ideas are made the starting point of philosophical thinking, as with Descartes (*Principia Philosophiae*, 1.13–19), the process of demonstrating God's existence becomes, like it or not, the unconvincing ontological argument.[11] With the earlier linguistic analysts, philosophy could deal with language about God, but not with his reality. Even Aristotle's reasoning from sensible things arrived at a plurality of finite substances, not an infinite creator. Aquinas' metaphysical procedure in demon-strating God's existence has been subject to various interpreta-tions in regard to the way its validity is to be sustained. In a word, the atheist can point to widespread disagreement among philosophers about the demonstration of God's existence. There is no theistic argument, taken just in itself, that will not be found challenged or rejected by an overwhelming majority in the philosophic world.

This situation need not be at all disconcerting to a profes-sional philosopher, for whom in the theoretical order authority is the weakest of arguments. What intelligence and reason show, not what authorities teach, guides his thought in his own field. But the situation indicates strongly enough that the be-liever has no obvious ground to presume that an atheist is deliberately going against reason, or against high ideals. The atheist may well be motivated by lofty objectives, such as the progress of mankind through science and culture. He may feel deep revulsion at what he considers the possible impeding of this progress by ignorance or by superstitious traditions. He may consider that he is in this way striving nobly to enhance human well-being. For profitable dialogue with him the believer needs to be keenly sensitive to these attitudes, and to realize sincerely that there is goodwill on his opponent's part. In this mutual respect there is common ground for the commencement of dialogue. Both sides claim to be struggling for the best. Both appeal to reason as their guide. Philosophically, each should be able to recognize the goodness and the rationality in the other. The pluralistic character of philosophy makes this possible. No matter how much a believer may disagree epistemologically with philosophies other than his own, he has to acknowledge their status as philosophy. By that fact he allows rationality to atheistic philosophies and plausibility to the atheist's refusal to accept theistic arguments with which even he himself disagrees. The atheist on his part has to face the pluralistic situation in philosophy, and realize that because some philosophies cannot give cogently demonstrative reasoning to the existence of God it does not follow that none can. Where rationality is allowed to both sides, debate on the issues is possible. Not the least of these issues will be that of human destiny.

From the viewpoint of the believer both himself and the nonbeliever are sharing, no matter how conflicting the ways, in the imperfect earthly stage of the same supernatural destiny. Each plays his part in the social life in which the journey to the supernatural goal is being undertaken. Each may honestly regard the other as sadly mistaken in understanding and outlook, and deceived in assessing the meaning and purpose of human life. But both can work together in bringing about the good they recognize in common in the intellectual and cultural and political spheres. Each from his respective viewpoint can make his contribution to the imperfect temporal happiness in which people, whether with or without explicit knowledge of it, are able to make their way towards the ultimate goal chosen for them by their creator.

The same overall attitude, though in significantly different fashion, is indicated where both sides of the dialogue are believers. Goodwill is to be presumed on the part of each. But here the worship of a higher personality brings a feeling of kinship into the discussion. This is especially relevant in the Jewish, Christian and Islamic approach with the express acknowledgement that all people are spiritual children of the one common father and share person-to-person relationship with him through divine revelation and providence. Mutual respect and love are called for by membership in the one common family. The belief that God speaks through grace to all who will hear him provides ample reason for listening to what each has to say. There is new sensitivity at present to a worldwide approach in this regard. Not only the sacred books of the Jewish, Christian, and Islamic traditions need to be taken into account, but also the religious aspirations and practices of all other peoples. Knowledge through affectivity has to be accorded its place. Along with the Scriptural formulations of the divine message, the promptings of divine grace in other religious manifestations merit attention. Both have their roles to play in the approach to the problems of human destiny today from the Christian viewpoint.

There need not be any doubt for the believer in regard to this universality of the divine promptings through the enlightenment of "every man born into the world" (Jn, 1.9), nor about the benefit of drawing spiritual profit and inspiration from the sight of virtuous conduct no matter where it is found. The sensitive consideration, rather, is the type of universality involved. Is it the kind that applies univocally to each instance, giving each the same essential status as a manifestation of divine truth? Or is it a universality based on focal meaning, in which divine revelation in its essential functioning is found in a primary instance only, and through focal reference in all other instances? Is religious truth subject to focal meaning somewhat like the aspect of existence in the philosophical order, or that of the sacred or numinous on the theological plane?

Assessed from the viewpoint of philosophy of religion, the actual situation seems clearly enough to fall into the Aristotelian framework of focal meaning. Each organized religious body quite naturally may be expected to proclaim that its own version of the Scriptural message is the true one. The pluralistic attitude of this type is familiar enough to the philosopher throughout his own general field. The human mind is so fashioned that it can accept different groups of naturally known propositions and build upon them in each case a different type of philosophy. Correspondingly, different sets of tenets can be accepted from divine revelation. Different religions and different theologies will be built upon them respectively. Each in the light of its own principles will consider the other to be in some way wrong. Yet for purposes of dialogue a common means of assessing the others is spontaneously sought, something to which all may in some way subscribe. The question of a general measure or standard or norm arises, through which the truth in each is to be gauged. Will this measure be something that is common in univocal fashion to all, in the way of a least common denominator? Or will it be the belief of one of the churches, acting as the primary instance by which the truth of all the others is measured according to the framework of focal meaning?

To determine what the norm for revealed truth is ranges far beyond the competence of philosophic consideration. It is a matter for religious faith. But with the different and clashing religious beliefs taken thematically as the subject matter of philosophy of religion, the question of how they are able to function harmoniously in the one ecumenical world and together play their roles in human destiny on earth, does face the philosopher. The Catholic philosopher approaches this problem with his own religious belief that the divine revelation upon which human destiny depends for its guidance has in its fullness been confided to a single church. This is a church that is one, holy, catholic, and apostolic in its nature.[12] To it has been given the office of safeguarding and interpreting the revealed doctrine of the Scriptures and of tradition. In its magisterium, through papal and conciliar infallibility, it can continue to serve in changing circumstances as the norm and measure of religious truth. What it teaches about itself in this regard indicates clearly enough the role of a living deposit of faith able to function vitally as the supreme earthly teacher of supernatural revelation. In these ways it marks itself off as what from a philosophical viewpoint may be regarded as the primary instance of the revealed truth, with all other instances dependent upon it in one way or another for the truth of what they profess.

In accord with the focal meaning framework, the sacredness of doctrines conserved elsewhere from this deposit are able to be recognized and appreciated by the Catholic faith. What is taught in other churches and religions in conformity with its various tenets is respected in virtue of intrinsic content.[13] Even where historical origins of religious doctrines antedate the Scriptures, their source in divine grace brings them under the notion of revealed truth and allows them to be viewed as secondary instances of it. In this way the Catholic thinker is able to see in the beliefs of others the same aspect of the sacred that he reveres in his own. The common belief in the Trinity and redemption is shared by him with other Christian churches. Belief in the sacramental life is shared with some. Worship of the one true God and belief in prayer is shared with Jews and Muslims. General reverence for the sacred is shared with many others. There is common recognition of moral goodness with atheists and agnostics. The Catholic has much common ground in varying grades, from his own point of view, to consort and dialogue with all other persons of goodwill and to merge with them in a common global life, enhancing the imperfect happiness in which human destiny is worked out on earth.

As theoretical philosophy, this view of the present religious situation expands smoothly enough. It sees the one church as catholic or universal in the sense of being the primary instance in the perspective of Aristotelian focal meaning, with the others sharing its religious teachings in differing degrees. As the primary instance of religious magisterium on earth, this church has the responsibility of preserving undiminished and unchanged the deposit of divine revelation. It cannot be expected to renounce or alter anything that it teaches to be essential to the deposit. Throughout all dialogue with other religious bodies this fundamental belief has to be kept intact and apparent. Here keen sensitivity to the feelings and reactions of all concerned is of prime importance. Ever present discernment and tact are required. Misunderstandings can easily arise. Happenings in the past can render participants purblind to the actual situation. Ingrained ways of viewing things need to be continually examined to be aware of what their origin really is and to what extent they are applicable to present conditions. Each problem has to be faced from all relevant angles, and right reason has indeed to work hard.

So faced, however, there is ample ground for urbane and profitable dialogue. From the Catholic side, much sacred truth can be seen in other religions. It can be discussed and applied to actual conduct. The rejection of further doctrinal or moral tenets has to be noted and the reasons for the rejection of them probed. This can be done tactfully and courteously. Without any personal animosity or triumphalistic attitude it can be made very clear that while from the Catholic viewpoint the rejection of these tenets is wrong, the good faith of people who do not see their way open to accepting them is not at all impugned. The office of preserving and interpreting the deposit of divine revelation in its fullness is not to be conceived as an imperialism holding dominion over palm and pine, but rather as a service to others in handing down the fullness of the revelation, a service to the servants of God to be freely accepted by them. Even when correctly understood, however, this magisterial office will be considered wrong by other churches and religious bodies. From the viewpoint of each side something faulty will therefore be seen in the other. But that need not hinder exchange of information on religious matters, and profit from each other's experiences, along with mutual help and encouragement in building up the temporal structure of human destiny on earth.

What is required here obviously, is tolerance. Tolerance does not mean accepting another's viewpoint as possibly correct. It means, rather, that the viewpoint is considered wrong. It is regarded as an evil, but an evil that is to be accepted for good reasons that are other than itself. St. Augustine wrote that it is part of the firmness of one's faith to put up with evils.[14] One's belief should be strong enough to bear with not only what one sees as different in the beliefs of others, but also with what one holds clearly and definitively to be erroneous in them. Where beliefs begin to infringe upon the rights of others or upon the common good, the question can become different. There the matter has to be settled by right reason, but with tolerance extended as far as possible. Locke, in advocating what for his time seemed extremely wide tolerance, made the reservation that "no opinions contrary to human society, or to those moral rules which are necessary to the preservation of civil society, are to be tolerated by the magistrate."[15] His particular examples of what could not be tolerated were a church whose members owed spiritual allegiance to a foreign prince, and atheists who undermine all religion and the possibility of the oaths upon which civil government depends. Locke could not see how an atheist could take an oath, or how anyone who owed spiritual allegiance to a foreigner could be trusted.[16] Yet today atheists and Muslims and Catholics are accepted without question as citizens. Experience and broader thinking have done away with those particular restrictions that seemed so necessary to Locke. Today wide-ranging thought and keen sensitivity to individual freedom and civil rights have given ample extension to the limits of tolerance. The good that justifies this openness is the exercise of human liberty.[17] It more than compensates, in the modern view, for the manifold evils that have to be tolerated.

The point in all this for Catholic philosophy of religion is that the good in other beliefs is to be recognized and the shortcomings tolerated. Reciprocally, other churches and religious bodies are expected to note what they see as good in Catholic belief and practice, and to tolerate what they consider to be evil. In this way, with right reason working out practical solutions for common action in each particular case, cooperative endeavor for building up the imperfect happiness of human destiny on earth may be carried on. On points where views differ, a Heraclitean clash of opposites may have its advantage in bringing forth a more dynamic type of action, and in guarding against the lethargy in which one good custom might corrupt the world.

In any case, from the standpoint of a primary instance of revealed truth, the secondary instances may always be regarded in two different ways. One is from the angle of the doctrine they share in focal reference. The other is from the viewpoint of what they lack from the full deposit of revelation. In the past, this second aspect tended to be emphasized far out of due proportion. An alleged tenet that error has no rights seemed popular. Strictly speaking, however, it is not a notion or a belief that has rights. It is the person who has the notion or holds the belief. The person, in virtue of the divinely bestowed gift of free will, has the right to hold and to do what he in the full exercise of his reason considers to be correct. Limits imposed by the common good, and the rights of others, have to be taken into consideration as right reason and public authority prescribe. But in practice today the range of toleration here is wide. If anything, still from the viewpoint of the primary instance, the danger to be guarded against is the diluting of the full deposit of revelation in the interests of ecumenical cooperation.

But even from the standpoint of other ecclesial bodies, diluting or watering down is not demanded in today's ecumenical spirit. Each such body is expected to hold what it believes and to work out ways of common activity with those whose beliefs are different. The tolerance can often be good-humored and witty, as when non-Catholic spokesmen, especially those with philosophical training, gently caricature the Catholic stand on papal infallibility. They expect it to be what it is, and not something that can be assimilated into a noninfallibility framework. Views contrary to one's own may be looked on as radically mistaken, without at all being taken as impediments to ecumenism. But sensitivity is imperative.

Finally, an older objection may sometimes be revived. The focal reference setting may be regarded as giving the primary instance an elevation that precludes the equality necessary for partners in a genuine debate. If the primary instance insists that it is already in possession of the full deposit of religious truth, the objection urges, it cannot be expected to see any point in listening to others. It has nothing to learn, and accordingly is not in a position to enter into profitable dialogue.

This objection fails to appreciate the way a primary instance is focally universal. The primary instance is universal without losing existential status in itself. Accordingly metaphysics can be a universal science without ceasing to exist as a science in itself over and against the other sciences. Failure to keep aware of that phase of universality through focal reference has kept modern commentators from seeing how Aristotle could conceive metaphysics as a theology with a particular type of being, the divine, as its object, while at the same time regarding it as a universal science, a science of being *qua* being that is not limited to any particular kind of being. Assessed outside the framework of focal meaning, this has appeared as an intolerable confusion. But in Aristotle himself theological science is universal because primary.[18] It is not universal through being severally identical with each one of the others, but by retaining its primary status as a science apart from all of them. They depend upon it for the scientific firmness and stability of their principles. It establishes and defends the principle of contradiction and the notions of truth and certainty upon which all other sciences depend. But by remaining a distinct science in its own right, it is able to learn from them and use information provided by them, for instance about the four causes and about the eternity of the world processes.[19] In an analogous way the church that holds itself to be the depository of the fullness of revealed truth can profit by learning about the ways particular instances of that truth have been put into practice by other religious bodies, and share with them its own experiences. The path to genuine dialogue and mutual assistance lies widely open.

For a philosophical approach to the problems arising from contemporary ecumenism, therefore, the technique of focal meaning is paramount. It provides the setting for mutual understanding and cooperation while allowing the integrity of the respective beliefs to be scrupulously maintained. Each religious body can regard the others as distinct units, each established in itself and sharing in one way or another in revealed truth. The truth each possesses has its worth as sacred. On its intrinsic merits it may be expected to lead ultimately in the right direction. Though for the time being the role is only ecumenical, it does not at all exclude the ultimate goal of full unity, even though for the moment the way in detail to that goal is not at all discernible. The "Lead Kindly Light" of Newman finds application and imparts encouragement wherever divine grace is at work in earthly living.[20]

V

As indicated by the foregoing considerations, there is no universal agreement in the contemporary world about what human destiny is. The liberal democracies leave the choice of it to the individual citizen. Marxist societies limit it strictly to this-worldly prosperity, by route of dictatorship that will finally disappear when the proper stage of indoctrination and attitudes has been reached. Where choice of destiny has been made according to Christian faith, its culmination has to be located beyond the present earthly life. Any philosophical outlook today that expressly excludes a life after bodily death, or that looks upon it as irrelevant to human action on earth, is incompatible with this concept of human destiny. As far as human destiny is being worked out upon earth, it consists expressly in a spiritual journey towards that goal. In today's liberal democracies the conditions can be brought about in which this journey may be taken with reasonable security and support. A philosophical estimate of the contemporary situation shows that believers have ample incentive to work together with nonbelievers to promote and ensure the maximum of the imperfect happiness that human destiny accords to man on earth.

As to the location of ultimate human destiny in contemplation, can the contemporary world be regarded as at all favorable? The overwhelming trend seems to prize external action. Pleasure, power and fame seem to dominate as goals, much as in Aristotle's times. Monasteries and convents are not as popular as they were in medieval days. Christian believers who strive to live for what their Gospels call the kingdom of God do not as a rule seem expressly to identify it with contemplation, even though they are familiar with its designation as the beatific vision and with the Scriptural texts telling them that eternal life means to see God face-to-face. There are eastern religions that still set a high value on contemplation as human destiny, and in the western world today many individuals feel the attraction of a contemplative life. But for the great majority of contemporary believers happiness seems to be conceived basically in terms of other attractions, and is extended in their religious belief to happiness without limit, usually left in general notions instead of being specified to contemplation. The rational development of the conception of human destiny as consisting essentially in theoretical contemplation is left rather to philosophy.

Philosophy of religion has in consequence the task of showing today how contemplation, for those who accept it as human destiny in the way revealed by the Scriptures, can satisfy to the full all human desires and can be one's eternal possession of all things in their highest way of existing. This is not an easy task in the contemporary world. The attractions of wealth, political and economic power, technological triumphs, career proficiency, and the cosy comforts and multiform diversions of an affluent society pull strongly in directions other than that of the course towards theoretical contemplation. The threat of nuclear holocaust, parental fear of the widespread ravages of drug addiction, the innate responsibility felt for the seemingly insoluble problems of hunger and want in sizable areas of the globe, tend to fix attention on questions deemed more practical.

Yet in comparison with former ages are the prospects any worse? The work ethic of the not so distant past, with its long hours of drudgery six days of the week, made the great majority of Western peoples much more the galley slaves of ongoing material aggrandizement than they are at present. Today's esteem for leisure and the attention to its requirements open horizons far wider than those of Vulcan, and provides the atmosphere for what Aristotle (*Metaph.*, 1.1,981b20–982a3) recognized as the necessary condition for theoretical engagement. The appreciation of intellectual life is implicit in the almost general opportunities now available for university education, in contrast to times when even secondary education was comparatively rare outside wealthy circles. Even though the thrust may be towards learning that can be put to external use in daily life, the attraction of knowledge for its own sake can hardly help but make itself felt with increasing effect. At least the opportunity is offered for proper esteem of intellection as a life. Fear of decimation by plagues, once as dreaded as nuclear destruction is today, has been obviated by medical competence. All in all, there is little reason to think that human destiny understood as the theoretical contemplation made known by revealed religion cannot be pursued as readily in the contemporary world as in any other epoch about which there is sufficient historical knowledge for making an accurate judgment. The divinely chosen destiny for man radiates its brilliance with the same all-pervasive intensity, and the task of probing its rationally accessible aspects and consequences continues to be a challenge for Catholic philosophy.

Epilogue

The preceding pages have taken a quick glance at some different conceptions of human destiny. They have noted in the Introduction that for Catholic belief the destiny of mankind is essentially the beatific vision of the triune God, with dynamic love and interpersonal activity following upon the intellection. This notion of human destiny is accepted on religious belief, and is intrinsically developed by sacred theology. But it poses a number of questions for a philosophically trained mind. To meet some of these, a philosophy that antedates Christianity and seems free from any direct influence of Hebraic revelation was examined in the book's first chapter. Aristotle's conclusions about human *eudaimonia* provided ground for understanding how one's destiny can as a full life consist essentially in intellection without lacking anything else required for it, and his epistemology showed how cognition is a means of possessing all things in the closest of possible unions. These considerations are crucial for encountering the philosophic problems that arise from belief in the beatific vision. In the second chapter a highly developed explanation of human destiny as it appeared in the relatively isolated Christendom of the Middle Ages was studied. In Aquinas the philosophical notions of Aristotle were found applied with success to the various relevant problems, and were moreover enhanced by a new metaphysics of existence. Finally,

79

in the third chapter consideration was given to philosophical problems about destiny that emerge in the present multicultural world insofar as it is divided most prominently between ideologies and liberal democracies. It is a world that exhibits widespread pluralism in both philosophy and religion, yet with the need to work out cooperatively a common temporal happiness.

This overview may seem to be dealing with only a sampling of the recorded notions bearing on human destiny. Quite other conceptions of it were developed in eastern cultures, in classical paganism, and in medieval speculations. Modern philosophies and contemporary religions offer different and variously nuanced views of it. But the notions just considered would seem to provide adequate philosophical means for facing the problems that arise most spontaneously from one's religious belief in the beatific vision as the destiny of mankind, and from the necessity of working cooperatively with others to achieve the good life upon earth as the temporal part of this destiny. In that setting philosophy has answers to a number of important queries.

These queries have been regarded as posed for *Catholic* philosophy. It is quite true that there is no unique type of thought corresponding to what has been called "officially Catholic philosophy."[1] Though Thomas Aquinas had been officially proposed by Leo XIII in the encyclical *Aeterni Patris* as the desired guide, the effort to bring Thomistic thought into a single philosophical system was not successful.[2] Aquinas has inspired many different ways of thinking, among his wide variety of readers. Further, numerous Catholic thinkers expressly reject his guidance, yet remain within the Catholic framework. Their various applications of philosophy to characteristically Catholic themes may all be designated as Catholic philosophy. Their common interests can give it that specification. But in the present context Aquinas is an especially apt guide. His way of demonstrating the existence of God can be shown to have meta-physical cogency, resting as it does upon the existence of sensible things as an actuality received ultimately from subsistent existence. It shows that God is a creator, and that he conserves in existence the things he has created, and that he concurs in all their activities.[3] Other arguments for the existence of God, such as the moral argument, the ontological argument, the argument from design, or the argument from universal consent, may have more persuasive appeal with numbers of people. But those arguments lack the metaphysical cogency required for philosophical demonstration here. Correspondingly Aquinas's demonstration of the indestructibility of the spiritual soul, based on the way the soul possesses its existence, is metaphysically cogent. These two conclusions, namely the existence of an infinite God and of an eternally indestructible soul, are the philosophical underpinnings for belief in a supernatural and everlasting destiny. True, the philosophical demonstrations are not at all essential for the individual in his personal religious belief. Nevertheless, they are a requisite for rational defense of the belief against one's own difficulties and the intellectual attacks by adversaries. They may be said to form an integral part of an intellectual believer's life. They deserve careful attention and preservation in our tradition.

The metaphysics upon which these two fundamental under-pinnings are evolved is adequate also for demonstrating how man's deepest aspirations and ultimate strivings can be satisfied by contemplation, provided the requisite object of intellection is accepted as religious faith teaches. It enables one to see rationally how anything else a person desires can be had in its fullness in the beatific contemplation, and in the highest and best way possible. It allows one to see how life here on earth is a type of happiness highly to be prized and to be worked for, because it is a happiness that gets its meaning as happiness from its orientation towards the supreme destiny known through revelation, namely the beatific vision of the Trinity. Further, in what the Aristotelian philosophy teaches about the growth and development of habituation, and in the Thomistic application of that teaching to grace, one is equipped to understand how life on earth is the way, the *via,* the habituation, towards the ultimate goal of man.

The thought of Aquinas, in consequence, is sufficient for guiding the mind to answers for philosophical questions that are occasioned by the Christian belief in human destiny. Other Catholic philosophies may have their own means of solving the problems that emerge in its regard. Those philosophies stand in their own right, and have to defend their own principles and methods. One purpose of the foregoing study has been to show that the problems can be met adequately by use of the philosophical principles found in Aquinas. Similarly other philosophies may have much to say about human happiness and destiny that could be applied with profit to these issues. In this regard the present survey has limited itself to the pagan thought of Aristotle, and has found in him a sufficient instance of how philosophy that is independent of Christian revelation can give the desired explanations and provide welcome solutions for certain problems arising from the revealed conception of human destiny.

Also the contemporary situation of liberal democracies vis-à-vis ideologies furnishes a sufficient sample of how the Catholic teaching on human destiny as something to be prepared on earth but achieved in fullness after bodily death, can function well enough in a geopolitical scene. With right reason the problems of dialogue and of practical cooperation can be solved. There is of course no room for naïveté. Here the divergences are deep, and passions can be violent. But with patience and goodwill on both sides, there are enough common objectives and common interests to allow possibility of practical settlement by right reason. Where the requisite freedom is allowed, believer can work with nonbeliever to build up the temporal good life that both are aiming at. In the framework of focal meaning the natural and the supernatural, the temporal and the eternal, can bring their endeavors into practical harmony.

The sampling, then, seems to have been sufficient for the purpose. The theme is vast, and invites much further investigation and study. But the general outlines of the philosophical problems arising from the religious conception of human destiny emerge clearly enough. No matter what type of Catholic philosophy is used to deal with them, the problems are serious and important. They call for adequate solution, in the traditional sense of faith seeking understanding. Rational safeguard is required for maintaining the intellectual nature of human destiny as vision, and for keeping intact the intimate connection of freedom with order during the journey towards it here on earth.[4] In these areas philosophy has a crucial role to play, even though it has no competence to question the religious beliefs in their own intrinsic status. Accordingly the present study has not attempted either to establish or to oppose the relevant beliefs. It has taken them as they are found professed by their respective adherents and has endeavored to outline the rational setting in which ecumenical enterprise may be carried on, and cooperation with nonbelievers for the achievement of temporal happiness can be assured.

In accord with this objective, the study has dealt with the way tolerance is to be understood and practiced in the common social and political life. Recognition of focal meaning in religious beliefs allows good to be seen in each, along with aspects that are regarded as evil. In focal meaning secondary instances can be set up against each other and against the primary instance. The good in each can be used as the basis for cooperation, while the other aspects can be tolerated for the sake of a greater good even though they are frankly held to be wrong. By neither side are truth and error given the same status. Merely a way of working together under different beliefs is set afoot, with the details being regulated by right reason. Each upholds his own stand as the truth, and rejects the opposite doctrine as error. But each respects the sincerity of the other, and acknowledges the sinfulness of coercion in an area that is meant for a free and generous acceptance of the morally good.

The difference of this procedure from that of sacred theology should be evident. Aquinas (*CG,* 1.2), with the explicit intention of defending the truth professed by the Catholic faith, and of banishing contrary errors, takes the method of arguing from Scriptural texts with those who accept the authority of either the old or the new testament. With those who accept neither, recourse to natural reason must be had. But natural reason, he recalls, is deficient in the realm of divine matters. That is the theological outlook. A philosophical method, on the other hand, can treat of divine matters without proceeding from divine principles.[5] It argues about revealed things without arguing from revealed tenets. In the present case its concern is not to debate whether beliefs are right or wrong. The concern is rather to show that belief in a supernatural destiny for mankind can be rationally defended against the objections of atheism and agnosticism, and that the various religious beliefs can consistently cooperate with each other and with atheists in building up the social structure and cultural settings requisite for temporal happiness. The procedure does not consist in proving one belief to be right and another to be wrong, but in showing rationally how all can live together. The difference from a theological procedure could hardly be made more evident. The subject matter is thematically religious, but the procedure is strictly philosophical. No appeal is made to any Scriptural authority or to the cognition of religious truths through affectivity. Yet no religious indifferentism or extreme philosophical relativism is inculcated. Rather, the one common real world is seen as basic for all.

The problems occasioned by the revealed doctrine of human destiny, then, may be approached on the strictly philosophical plane by a Catholic thinker who is firm in his religious belief. The belief places human destiny primarily and essentially in beholding the substance of the triune God for all eternity after bodily death, and secondarily in the journey towards that goal during life on earth. This belief poses notable problems for Catholic philosophy.

First and foremost, there are the queries about contemplation. Readily seen, perhaps, is the necessity of cognition for any kind of specifically human good, since what one does not perceive or know gives neither pleasure nor satisfaction. But to realize how cognition in its highest degree can contain in itself every other human good requires philosophical effort. The cognition experienced on earth is never directly of itself. It is always of some other object. The thing perceived or known dominates. The worth of cognition just in itself is easily missed. Secondly, there are the problems regarding the temporal part of human destiny. These concern the difficulties encountered in always transcending the outlook of the present time, yet always working cooperatively with others whose outlooks differ. Queries keep continually arising. They demand philosophical reflection for their answers.

In these respects, an habituation through grace renders the acceptation of revealed truths comparatively easy for a Catholic thinker. But it does not in the least dull his urge to understand their rational aspects. In discussion, however, he has to keep in mind that others are habituated differently. They find many of his beliefs extremely hard to tolerate, let alone accept. Aristotle (*Metaph.*, 2.3,994b32–995a6) noted how deeply the habituation one has received affects one's philosophical thinking, even in theoretical matters. The history of philosophy bears out this observation abundantly, as Platonists, Aristotelians, Thomists, Scotists, Kantians, Hegelians, Marxists, pragmatists, phenomenologists, analysts, and countless others go their respective ways. It is of the utmost importance that the all-pervasive influence of the different types of habituation be kept carefully in view throughout the efforts to achieve the imperfect happiness of human destiny on earth. Perfection is not to be expected.

Even habituation through grace does not bring about anything like the thoroughgoing harmony one would like to see in human enterprises on earth. "How odd of God" is often the natural reaction to the ways in which divine grace calls and leads people. One spontaneously expects those ways to correspond exactly with one's own ways. Here the philosophical conclusions about the finitude of human wisdom and about the infinity of the divine wisdom, of the divine power and of the divine mercy, serve as a strong underpinning for tolerance. They help restrain the quick desire to call down fire from heaven (Lc 9.54–56) on those who will not accept one's own views. They temper the impulse to cut away the wheat along with the chaff long before the harvest time (Mt 13.24–30). Along with his severe condemnation the first efficient cause of all things keeps imparting his concurrence even to the most evil of acts. No instant annihilation takes place by way of retribution. Possession of the means for suppression does not necessarily call for their use. Ample room for tolerance is allowed.

In numerous areas, then, belief in the supernatural destiny preached by Christian faith can be supported intellectually by philosophy of religion. Even apart from this practical help the understanding spontaneously sought by faith is a boon in its own right. At the beginning of the *Metaphysics* Aristotle sig-

nalized the natural desire of everyone to know, and focused the
desire on the highest causes of things, including the final cause.
Need there be any wonder that this natural desire for knowledge
should prove highly operative in regard to one's ultimate destiny?

NOTES AND REFERENCES

INTRODUCTION

[1] The responsibility of everyone to work towards and keep "faith in the high destiny of Man" was stressed by Pierre Lecomte du Noüy, *Human Destiny* (New York: Longmans, Green and Co., 1947), p. viii. Cf. "Let every man remember that the destiny of mankind is incomparable and that it depends greatly on his will to collaborate in the transcendent task." Ibid., p. 273. The central role of human destiny for understanding in depth the natural world and all reality has been expressed in the reflection, "Man is not a fragmentary part of the world but contains the whole riddle of the universe and the solution of it," Nicolas Berdyaev, *The Destiny of Man*, trans. Natalie Duddington (London: Geoffrey Bles, 1937; reprint, 1959), p. 45. This implies that through man the rest of the observable universe attains its overall destiny. The topics thereby involved are as a rule treated under teleology, ethics, or the philosophy of man. But in various languages and literary formats they have been made the subject for separate monographs under the caption of human destiny, as in Fichte's *Die Bestimmung des Menschen* (Berlin: Vossischen Buchhandlung, 1800); John Fiske, *The Destiny of Man* (Boston: Houghton, Mifflin, 1884); Georges A. Rubissow, *Le destin*, trad. Nina Nidermiller (Paris: La Palatine, 1965); *The Destiny of Man*, ed. Rischabhchand and Shyamsundar Jhunjhunwala (Pondicherry: Sri Aurobindo Society, 1969); Juan Antonio Ortega y Medina, *Destino Manifiesto* (México: Secretaría de Educación Pública, 1972). There are numerous works under the title of the destiny of particular cities and countries and continents and civilizations and races, of languages and literatures, of drama and the

theater, of metaphysics and of the philosopher, and of fire, gold, the dollar, and so on. All in all, they testify abundantly to the fascinating appeal the notion of destiny naturally evokes.

[2] The term *ideology* first appeared in 1798, coined by a French nobleman in the effort to rebuild civilization after the turmoil of the French revolution. See Antoine-Louis-Claude Destutt de Tracy, *Eléments d'idéologie,* 3rd ed. (Paris: Courcier, 1817; Reprint, Paris: Vrin, 1970), 1: 11 (Gouhier's "Introduction historique"). The notion of "ideas" as contained in it goes back through Condillac and Locke to Descartes. The ideas were explicitly the ideas of the human mind as objects of consideration.

[3] Cf.: "For it is my Father's will that everyone who looks upon the Son and puts his faith in him shall possess eternal life." Jn 6.40. "This is eternal life: to know thee who alone art truly God, and Jesus Christ, whom thou hast sent." Jn 17.3. ". . . then we shall see face to face. My knowledge is now partial, then it will be whole, like God's knowledge of me." I Cor 13.12. Trans. *The New English Bible* (Cambridge: University Press, 1961).

[4] William Ernest Henley, *I. M., R. T. Hamilton Bruce,* in *Echoes,* IV.

[5] A good synopsis may be found in William P. Alston, s.v. "Philosophy of Religion, Problems of," in *The Encyclopedia of Philosophy* (ed. Paul Edwards). On religious fact as a phenomenon, see Zofia J. Zdybisca, "Man and Religion," in M. A. Krapiec's *I-Man,* trans. M. Lescoe, A. Woznicki, T. Sandok et al. (New Britain, Conn.: Mariel Publications, 1983), pp. 277–305. The situation has been expressed bluntly as "Philosophy of religion is that philosophy whose subject matter is—religion." Yitzhak Julius Guttmann, *On the Philosophy of Religion* (Jerusalem: Hebrew University, 1976), p. 11. Its aim is "to understand religion as a phenomenon" (ibid.). On the inherent difficulties in the notion of the philosophy of religion, see Antoine Vergote, "La religion comme épreuve paradoxale pour la philosophie," in *La philosophie de religion,* ed. Enrico Castelli (Paris: Aubier, 1977), pp. 21–35. The alien character of its object is noted: "La philosophie, en effet, ne peut reconnaître comme proprement religieuse que la religion qui est en dehors des limites de la raison. L'ayant reconnue comme l'autre, elle peut se mettre à son écoute, reprendre du dedans

ses significations, contribuer à en élucider les articulations" (p. 35). Modern treatises on the philosophy of religion are numerous, e.g.,: Edgar Sheffield Brightman, *A Philosophy of Religion* (New York: Prentice-Hall, 1940); David Elton Trueblood, *Philosophy of Religion* (New York: Harper & Brothers, 1957); James Collins, *The Emergence of Philosophy of Religion* (New Haven: Yale University Press, 1967); Maxwell John Charlesworth, *Philosophy of Religion* (London: Macmillan, 1972); Brian Davies, *An Introduction to the Philosophy of Religion* (Oxford: Oxford University Press, 1982). Bibliographies may be found in Brightman, pp. 490–522, Collins, pp. 492–506, and Davies, pp. 140–142. The attitude in philosophy of religion towards doctrines professed on religious belief has been concisely stated as: "To sum up, then, the philosopher of religion is not expected to pronounce either for or against the truth of the religious claim that is explicit or implicit in the theophany . . . the philosopher of religion does not decide upon the ultimate truth of the claims made by a religion." Kenneth L. Schmitz, "World and Word in Theophany," *Faith and Philosophy,* 1 (1984): 59. On a parallel view in Aquinas, see infra, Epilogue, n. 5.

⁶"Et tenent philosophi perfectionem naturae, et negant perfectionem supernaturalem; theologi vero cognoscunt defectum naturae et necessitatem gratiae et perfectionem supernaturalem." John Duns Scotus, *Ord.,* Prol., 1.1.5; ed. Vaticana, I, 4.14–17. In the context Scotus was speaking of the pagan philosophers in the Peripatetic tradition. Yet even in medieval times the term "philosopher" could be applied in various senses to Christian writers. On the conception of Christians as "philosophers," see Martin Grabmann, "Ist das 'philosophische Universalgenie' bei Magister Heinrich dem Poeten Thomas von Aquin?" *Historisches Jahrbuch,* 38 (1917): 315–320. On the natural lack of full comprehension of human destiny in this regard, one might compare with Scotus' assertion the words of Fichte: "Meine ganze, vollständige Bestimmung begreife ich nicht; was ich werden soll, und was ich sein werde, übersteigt alles mein Denken." *Die Bestimmung des Menschen,* (reprint; Hamburg: Felix Meiner, 1972), p. 145. Aristotle had remarked (*Metaph.,* 6.1,1026a27–29; 11.7,1064b9–14) that if there were no other substances over and above nature, philosophy of nature would be the highest kind of

philosophy; but if there is a higher kind of being than nature, then the philosophy that deals with it will be the highest. From the Christian viewpoint one might add that if there were no state for man higher than that of nature, philosophy would be the highest in the list of sciences; but if there is supernatural elevation, the cognition that has it as its object will be the requisite for a comprehensive grasp of human destiny.

[7] Statistics in this regard can of course be only approximate, and the estimates vary considerably. A recent summary may be found in the editorial "A Few Figures," *Lumen Vitae,* 39 (1984): 7–9. It places (p. 9) the sum total of Jews, Christians, and Muslims at about 45 percent of the world's population.

CHAPTER ONE

[1] See Aristotle, *Metaph.,* 12.9,1074b35–1075a9; *De an.,* 3.8, 431b20–432a9. In current secondary literature the blackout on positive treatment of this epistemology is almost total. I have tried to survey its meaning and history, and emphasize its relevance, in some articles collected in *Aristotle,* ed. John R. Catan (Albany: State University of New York Press, 1981), pp. 59–108. On the notion "theoretical," see infra, n. 13.

[2] These three collections are named respectively the *Nicomachean Ethics,* the *Eudemian Ethics,* and the *Magna Moralia.* On their history, interrelation, chronology, and relative importance the secondary literature is extensive. See Franz Dirlmeier, *Aristoteles: Magna Moralia* (Berlin: Akademie Verlag, 1958), pp. 93–147; Anthony Kenny, *The Aristotelian Ethics* (Oxford: Clarendon Press, 1978), pp. 1–59; 215–239.

[3] See Aristotle, *E N,* 6.2,1139a31. Cf. *Metaph.,* 6.1,1025b2–24. On the guidance of choice by practical wisdom, see *E N,* 6.8–13,1141b23–1145a11; *Metaph.,* 11.8.1065a32.

[4] *E N,* 1.1,1094a1–3. The notion of the good as the end of all the sciences is repeated at *E N,* 1.6,1097a4–5, and is found at *M M,* 1.1,1182a32–36, and at *Pol.,* 3.12,1282b14–15. The description of it as that at which all things aim is repeated at *E N,* 1.4,1095a14–15,

and given also at *Rh.*, 1.6,1362a23. At *E N*, 10.2,1172b9–15, the dictum is attributed to Eudoxus, in reference to "rational and irrational" beings. On the background in Plato, see *Phlb.* 20D, 22B, and *Grg.*, 499E–500A.

⁵See John Burnet, *The Ethics of Aristotle* (London: Methuen, 1900), p. 1.

⁶"Destiny," as "that which is destined or fated to happen" *O.E.D.*, s.v., can be either good or bad. The *Enciclopedia Filosofica* merely refers to its entry "Fatalismo" for the notion. Yet "fate" (the Greek *heimarmenê*—see LSJ, s.vv. *meiromai* and *Moira*) suggests something over which one has no control, while "destiny" extends to something one can work out for oneself. For Aristotle (*E N*, 1.9,1100a5–9) a man like Priam does not attain *eudaimonia*, yet (1.10,1100b28–1101a13) by exercising great virtue he keeps from becoming miserable. From the viewpoint of the present study, he can maintain his high destiny as a man, even though fate treats him so cruelly. On the etymological meaning of destiny as something fixed and stable, see Ernout-Meillet, s.v. **-stano (sto)*.

⁷For the use of this translation, see John M. Cooper, *Reason and Human Good in Aristotle* (Cambridge, Mass.: Harvard University Press, 1975), pp. 89–90.

⁸E.g., *E N*, 1.7,1098a19; 8,1100a32–b2. One might compare the English "bliss" and "blessedness," both applicable to supreme beatitude even though their etymologies are radically different.

⁹This life of public standing is not to be confused with the life of practical virtue (*E N*, 10.8,1178a9–b7), which is genuine *eudaimonia* though in a secondary fashion, and is based on virtue while prestige as the motivation is not. The glamor of public recognition becomes the driving force in the life that Aristotle here rejects.

¹⁰A discussion of this translation may be found in my paper "The ΚΑΛΟΝ in the Aristotelian *Ethics*," in *Studies in Aristotle*, ed. Dominic J. O'Meara (Washington, D.C.: The Catholic University of America Press, 1981), pp. 264–269. Lloyd P. Gerson, "The Aristotelianism of Joseph Owens," *Ancient Philosophy*, 3 (1983): 81, n. 42, contrasts this with my use elsewhere of "seemly" as the translation of *kalon*. Neither English word does full justice to the Aristotelian term.

Each emphasizes one aspect of it. Both the attractive glow of the *kalon* and its obligatory character have to be kept in mind together, with the one or the other stressed according to the context in which it is being used.

[11] Cicero, *Tusc. Disp.*, 5.3.9; Diogenes Laertius, *Lives*, 8.8.

[12] Cf. the lines of Robert Service in "The Spell of the Yukon," *Complete Poems* (New York: Dodd, Mead & Company, 1935), p. 18:

> Yet it isn't the gold that I'm wanting
> So much as just finding the gold.

On "as good as gold" Francis E. Sparshott, *An Enquiry into Goodness* (Toronto: University of Toronto Press, 1958), p. 158, aptly quotes from Belloc's epigram *Fatigue* the line "Money gives me pleasure all the time." In Aristotle's reasoning, however, neither the money itself nor the activity of acquiring the money can be naturally an end in itself, since by their nature they are both but means to something further. The type of goodness they offer, formally as money and its pursuit, is in actual fact not the goodness of an end but only of a means.

[13] *Metaph.*, 6.1.1025b18–28. In this context "theoretical" does not have the modern sense of hypothetical or untested. It is used in the ancient Greek signification in which *theoria* meant contemplation just for the sake of contemplation, as in the esthetic contemplation of a work of art such as a sculpture by Phidias. Its object was already there to be known. Contrasted with it in Aristotle (*Cael.*, 3.7,306a16–17; *P.A.*, 1.1,640a3–4) from this viewpoint of having an object already there and appearing before it, was productive science whose object was yet to be made. Similarly the object of practical science was something yet to be done.

[14] On deliberation, see Aristotle, *E N*, 3.3,1112a18–1113a14. A discussion may be found in Cooper, pp. 1–88. On the responsibility for one's own actions, see *E N*, 3.5,1113b3–1114b25. A discussion of the role of right reason in Aristotle may be found in my paper "How Flexible is Aristotelian 'Right Reason,'" in *The Georgetown Symposium of Ethics*, ed. Rocco Porreco (Lanham, Md.: University Press of America,

1984), pp. 49–65. In contrast to luck, "choice does not exist apart from thinking" (*Metaph.*, 11.8,1065a32).

[15] On the "intrinsic worth" of a moral action in the Aristotelian teleology, see Henry B. Veatch, "Telos and Teleology in Aristotelian Ethics," in *Studies in Aristotle* (supra, n. 10), pp. 279–296. On "obligatory ends," see ibid., pp. 281–291.

[16] *E N*, 1.5,1095b15. On the meaning, see John Alexander Stewart, *Notes on the Nicomachean Ethics*, (Oxford, Clarendon Press, 1892), I: 58–59. Its sense is "being derived, as is only natural, from their own experience of life." It does not imply *"our inference"* from the way they live, but their own derivation of the notion of goodness from the habituation they have developed. The point at issue is the *proportion* between the habituation and the ultimate goal chosen on its account. The *kalon* experienced in secondary instances adapts a person to desire it in its primary instance.

[17] *De an.*, 2.12,424a17–b12; 3.4,429b5–10; 8,431b21–432a3.

[18] See Aquinas, *Quodl.*, 8.1. Text infra, Chapter Two, nn. 22–23.

[19] On this allegedly "broad, indeed commonsense, conception," see Cooper, pp. 147–149.

[20] See G. E. L. Owen, "Logic and Metaphysics in Some Earlier Works of Aristotle," in *Aristotle and Plato in the Mid-Fourth Century,* ed. Ingemar Düring and G. E. L. Owen (Göteborg: Studia Graeca et Latina Gothoburgensia, 1960), p. 169. On the problem whether the characteristic predicated by focal reference is intrinsic to the secondary instances, see infra n. 27.

[21] For Aristotle (*Metaph.*, 4.2,1003b12–15) what is said of things through focal reference *(pros hen)* is in its own way said of them universally *(kath' hen)*. In Pseudo-Alexander (*In Metaph.*, pp. 447.22–32; 661.33–39) Aristotle is interpreted explicitly as making use in this way of two different kinds of universality.

[22] On this topic, see Ralph McInerny, "The Nature of Book *Delta* of the *Metaphysics* According to the Commentary of Saint Thomas Aquinas," in *Graceful Reason,* ed. Lloyd P. Gerson (Toronto: Pontifical Institute of Mediaeval Studies, 1983), pp. 334–342.

[23] B. A. G. Fuller, "The Theory of God in Book Λ of Aristotle's *Metaphysics,*" *Philosophical Review,* 16 (1907): 176.

²⁴ For the suggestion of "a supernatural urge" (p. 207), see Francis H. Parker, "Contemplation in Aristotelian Ethics," in *The Georgetown Symposium on Ethics* (supra, n. 14), pp. 207–209. In reading Aristotle's descriptions of separate substance, one feels that they do not come just from abstract reasoning. They seem like intuition based upon cognition through activity by grace, or upon some kind of mystical knowledge. Both those origins exceed a purely philosophical approach. On the "connaissance affective de Dieu" as speculative knowledge, and as coming under the object of sacred theology, see Rafael-Tomas Caldera, *Le jugement par inclination chez saint Thomas d'Aquin* (Paris: Vrin, 1980), p. 135.

²⁵ For the meaning of this difficult text, see W. D. Ross, *Aristotle's Metaphysics* (Oxford: Oxford University Press, 1948), 2: 398–399. The last line can be translated at least equally well as "it does not have the good in this or that instance, but in a whole. . . ."

²⁶ See *De an.*, 2.4,415a26–b7; *G A*, 2.1,731b31–35.

²⁷ Aristotle's standard examples of health and medicine might at first thought suggest that secondary instances have no genuine being intrinsically in themselves. Health as a nature is not intrinsic to cooked spinach, or to exercise, or to color. Nor is medical science intrinsic to a scalpel or to a campus building. Aristotle in using those examples was intent on showing that the primary instance of being is really a different thing from the secondary instances. It is not intrinsic to them in the way that "a man" in its full nature is severally intrinsic to each human person. Things in other categories are beings through reference to substance, and sensible substances are beings through reference to immaterial substances. By virtue of its own nature each thing is *what* it is in itself—a man, an animal, a horse, an ox, a color, a size, a grammarian. That is the nature of each. But each is a being through reference to something outside its own nature, and ultimately to separate form. Substance is not in any category of accident, nor are immaterial beings intrinsic to sensible substance. At first sight the Aristotelian focal meaning would seem to prevent the aspect referred to from being present intrinsically in the secondary instances.

Nonetheless for Aristotle "*being a man* and *a man* are the same" (*Metaph.*, 4.2,1003b26–27; Apostle trans.). The Stagirite seems quite obviously to mean that just as unity and being, while really the same, differ in concept but would be more advantageously represented for the present purpose as conceptually identical, so being and thing though conceptually different can in focal meaning be more helpfully regarded as identical with each other in every particular instance. This is the way truth and being were assessed in *Metaph.*, 2.1,993b24–31. Each thing had truth to the extent it had being. Both characteristics were possessed in the highest degree by the primary instance and caused by it in the secondary instances. A fragment from *On Philosophy* (*Fr.* 15,1476b23–24), moreover, uses the argument from degrees in beings to prove the existence of a best: "Since, then, among existing things one is better than another, there is also something best, which will be the divine" (trans. Ross, *Fr.* 16; *The Works of Aristotle,* 12: 87–88). This is applied to the *kalon* at b32–34. What has been called the "attenuation of predicates," Terence Penelhum, *Religion and Rationality* (New York: Random House, 1971), p. 148, does not in this case begin with the perfection in the highest degree and attempt to attenuate it into lower degrees. It begins rather with the perfection as known in various degrees in sensible things, as, here, the way being is known in substances and in accidents. From those lower degrees the reasoning goes to the far higher degree in the primary instance. The varying degrees in the secondary instances are observed as a fact, and the primary instance, in which the perfection exists in its own nature, is inferred. But there is no attempt to make the primary conform to the secondary instances, as in asking how perfections in God can contain the special traits they have in creatures. Rather, the secondary have to conform as far as possible to the primary.

In a word, for Aristotle the focal reference in secondary instances can be either to a primary instance that is really different in nature from them and remains entirely extrinsic to them, or to a primary instance that is the nature of a perfection possessed by them intrinsically in themselves in imperfect or attenuated degrees. In regard to being, the examples of health and medicine were used to emphasize the real difference of the *primary* from the secondary instances, while leaving intact the question whether the characteristic in its *secondary* instances can in some way be really identical with the nature of the things it characterizes in these instances. While its primary instance is really different from all other instances, each secondary instance may nevertheless be identical with some other nature. With Aquinas, for whom being and thing are always really distinct in secondary instances, no problem arises in this regard. For him, being is a nature in God alone. In all other things it is really distinct from their natures, and is graded according to those natures. But in Aristotle things and their being are really identical, making a gradated structure much harder to understand. Here as elsewhere loose ends are left untied by the Stagirite. He follows the facts as far as they were apparent to him, without forcing them into philosophical systematization.

The heritage left by Aristotle was in that way incomplete—quite as the nature upon which it is built is incomplete when viewed by the Christian theologian. But it remained open. The light struck by the spark continued to glow. Plotinus (*En.*, 3.8.4,39–47) and the long tradition of Neoplatonism kept alive the superior status of contemplation, assessing both action in the external world and the production of material things as weakness of contemplation or meant merely to accompany it, and as suitable for duller types. Through this tradition in Christian Neoplatonism, and later through a direct contact with the Aristotelian writings, the Scriptural location of human destiny in vision was able to enjoy philosophical attendance.

CHAPTER TWO

¹ "Unde inter alia quae homines de sapiente concipiunt, a Philosopho ponitur quod *sapientis est ordinare.*" Aquinas, *CG,* 1.1, Multitudinis. Cf. Aristotle, *Metaph.,* 1.2,982a17–18. In Aristotle the contrast is with the wise man giving orders and the others receiving them *(epitattesthai).* Aquinas' application of the Aristotelian dictum in the sense of putting order into the subject matter of the sciences may be seen in the reason he gives: "Cuius ratio est quia sapientia est potissima perfectio rationis, cuius proprium est cognoscere ordinem." *Sent. Eth.,* 1.1.1; *Op. Om.,* ed. Leon., 47: 3.2–4.

² "Finis autem ultimus uniuscuiusque rei est qui intenditur a primo auctore vel motore ipsius. Primus autem auctor et motor universi est

intellectus, ut infra ostendetur. Oportet igitur ultimum finem universi esse bonum intellectus." *CG*, 1.1., Finis.

³ "Hoc autem est veritas. Oportet igitur veritatem esse ultimum finem totius universi. . . . Sed et Primam Philosophiam Philosophus determinat esse *scientiam veritatis;* non cuiuslibet, sed eius veritatis quae est origo omnis veritatis, scilicet quae pertinet ad primum principium essendi omnibus; unde et sua veritas est omnis veritatis principium; sic enim est dispositio rerum in veritate sicut in esse." *CG*, 1.1, Finis. "Truth" here is taken in the sense in which it is coextensive with being, as in Aristotle, *Metaph.*, 1.2,993b26–31. On "focal" order, cf. supra, Chapter One, n. 20.

⁴ There is wide disagreement on the interpretation of Aquinas' "ways" for demonstrating the existence of God. For the three ways mentioned in *Sent.*, 1.3, div. lae partis textus (ed. Mandonnet, 1: 88), the probative force of the demonstration is explicitly based on the reception of a creature's being *(esse)* from another. For the case that this holds equally for the "five ways" of the *Summa Theologiae* and of the *Contra gentiles*, see my article "Aquinas and the Five Ways," *The Monist*, 58 (1974): 16–35.

⁵ Cf. *ST*, 1.2.2,c and ad 3m.; *CG*, 1.12. From the existence of sensible things as caused existence the demonstration shows that existence subsists in a primary instance. Existence is then seen to be the nature of that primary instance, because in this unique case it is what subsists.

⁶ "Non est igitur possibile ad hanc visionem perveniri ab aliquo intellectu creato nisi per actionem divinam." *CG*, 3.52, Adhuc.

⁷ ". . . ea quae supra rationem in ultimo hominum fine expectantur, sicut resurrectio et glorificatio corporum, perpetua beatitudo animarum, et quae his connectuntur." *CG*, 4.1, Quia vero.

⁸ "Sed quia perfectum hominis bonum est ut quoquo modo Deum cognoscat, ne tam nobilis creatura omnino in vanum esse videretur, velut finem proprium attingere non valens, datur homini quaedam via per quam in Dei cognitionem ascendere possit." *CG*, 4.1, Intellectus. Cf.: "Perfectio autem spiritualis naturae in cognitione veritatis consistit." *De ver.*, 15.1, Resp.; ed. Leon., 22: 479.270–271.

[9] "Tertia est secundum quod mens humana elevabitur ad ea quae sunt revelata perfecte intuenda." *CG,* 4.1, Est.

[10] See Anton C. Pegis, "Nature and Spirit: Some Reflections on the Problem of the End of Man," *Proceedings of the American Catholic Philosophical Association,* 23 (1949): 62–97, on the tenet that "the nature of man is naturally endless" (p. 73). The controversy was set afoot by Henri de Lubac, *Surnaturel* (Paris: Aubier, 1946). De Lubac, *The Mystery of the Supernatural,* trans. Rosemary Sheed (London: Geoffrey Chapman, 1967), p. 65, emphasized that "God can never be under any obligation, any sort of requirement, to give himself to the being he has made." For a survey of the controversy at the time, see P. Donnelly, "Current Theology," *Theological Studies,* 8 (1947): 483–491; 9 (1948): 213–249, 554–560.

[11] See text cited supra, Introduction, n. 6.

[12] ". . . velut causa quaedam profundens totum ens et omnes eius differentias." *In Periherm.,* 1.14.22. The objection, nevertheless, may still be heard on the popular level on the part of professed atheists that the mention of God in a nation's constitution negates all the rights and liberties it guarantees. On the philosophical level, the much debated question of the divine liberty versus natural necessity is wrongly placed. Liberty is a perfection, found in its highest instance in God, while necessity and contingence of action are both on a lower level. The question should be regarded as concerned with a divine action that is free, as are all divine actions bearing upon an external object, but also not contingent.

[13] ". . . ipsa maiestas divina videbitur, et omnis bonorum perfectio." *CG,* 4.1, Quod vero subdit, *Quis.*

[14] ". . . partakers of the divine nature." II Pt, 1.4.

[15] " . .postquam uero usum rationis habent, tenentur salutis sue curam agere. Quodsi fecerint, iam absque peccato originali erunt, gratia superveniente; si vero non fecerint, talis omissio est eis peccatum mortale." Aquinas, *De malo,* 5.2, ad 8m; ed. Leonine, 23: 135a. On the topic see Salmanticenses, *Cursus Theologicus,* 14.6.2.2.43–45 and 14.6.3.7.103–107; (Paris: Palmé, 1878), 9:751–753 and 785–787.

[16] "Post baptismum autem necessaria est homini jugis oratio, ad hoc quod caelum introeat." *St,* 3.39.5,c. Cf. 2–2.83.2.

[17] Although in the *Sed contra* of *ST,* 2–2.64.2, Aquinas cites the authority of Scripture for punishment by death, in the body of the article he argues as though it were a matter of right reason and natural law, God being the author of the eternal law of which the natural law is a participation. But as regards the command given to Abraham to sacrifice Isaac, Aquinas (*ST,* 2–2.64.6, ad 1m) appeals to the person-to-person command of God who has dominion over life and death. The death penalty for Ananias and Saphira is likewise justified (64.4, ad 1m) on the ground of the same divine dominion.

[18] ". . . omnes qui recte senserunt posuerunt finem humanae vitae Dei contemplationem. Contemplatio autem Dei est duplex. Una per creaturas, quae imperfecta est, ratione jam dicta, in qua contemplatione Philosophus, X *Ethic.,* cap. ix, felicitatem contemplativam posuit, quae tamen est felicitas viae." Aquinas, *Sent.,* Prol. 1.1, Solut.; ed. Mandonnet, 1:7–8. Cf. *CG,* 3.37, Ad hanc etiam omnes. On the theological concept of early life as a *via,* see Gerhart B. Ladner, "*Homo Viator:* Medieval Ideas on Alienation and Order," *Speculum,* 42 (1967): 233–259.

[19] "Unde oportet ut ea quae sunt ad finem proportionentur fini, quatenus homo manducatur ad illam contemplationem in statu viae per cognitionem non a creaturis sumptam sed immediate ex divino lumine inspiratam." Aquinas, *Sent.,* Prol. 1.1, Solut.; 1:8.

[20] "Unde duo notantur in verbis praedictis; scilicet praeparatio, quae est per sacramenta, et inductio in gloriam." *Sent., Prol.* S. Thomae; 1:4. But for every morally good action, conformity with prudence and right reason is required. Cf. *ST,* 1–2.63.3,c; 2–2.47.7,c.

[21] David Hume, *Enquiries concerning Human Understanding and Concerning the Principles of Morals,* 9.1.219; 3rd ed. L. A. Selby-Bigge, rev. P. H. Nidditch (Oxford: Clarendon Press, 1975), p. 270.

[22] "Unde uniuscuiusque naturae causatae *prima* consideratio est secundum quod est in intellectu divino; *secunda* vero consideratio est ipsius naturae absolute; tertia secundum quod habet esse in rebus ipsis, vel in mente angelica; *quarta* secundum esse quod habet in

intellectu nostro." *Quodl.,* 8.1.1,c. Cf. *Sent.,*1.36.1.3, ad 1m; 1: 836–837. See infra, n. 24, for texts on God as the existence of all things.

[23]"Sic autem senarius non erit creatura, sed ratio creaturae in creatore, quae est idea senarii; et est idem secundum rem quod divina essentia, ratione tantum differens." *Quodl.,* 8.1.1,c. Cf.: "quia creaturae in Deo sunt causatrix essentia, ut dicit Anselmus. . . ." *Sent.,*1.36.1.3, ad 1m; 1: 836. Cf. Anselm, *Monol.,* 34–36. One might also compare Augustine, *De Trin.,* 4.1.3; ed. W. J. Mountain, p. 162.40–44.

[24]See *Sent.,* 1.8.1.2.; 1: 197–198; *CG,* 1.26. *ST,* 1.3.8, ad 1m; 1.4.2,c.

[25]See *De an.,* 3.5,430a23–25. For Aristotle (1.4,408b27–29) remembering was an activity of the composite of soul and body, a composite that perished in death.

[26]See *Q. de an.,* 14; *De immortalitate animae,* ed. L. A. Kennedy, in *Archives d'histoire doctrinale et littéraire du moyen âge,* 45 (1978): 209–223.

[27]*ST,* 1.44.1; 45.1–5; 104.1–2; 105.5.

[28]Supra, n. 18. On the part played by bodily life, see also *ST,* 1-2.3.3, and *Sent.,* 4.1.3.qa 5.Solut.2, ad 1m; ed. Vivès, 11: 468a.

CHAPTER THREE

[1]See supra, Chapter Two, n. 18. The deep difference in this approach from that of secular philosophy is not to be underestimated. Yet in the present ecumenical atmosphere and the revived interest in religious thought there is no need for the disheartened feeling expressed more than two decades ago by the then seventy-five-year-old Etienne Gilson, as he looked back over his philosophical career: "But he who philosophizes as a Christian feels himself more hopelessly isolated, especially in the middle of this twentieth century and its deeply dechristianized environment. It is trying and, in the long run discouraging, to go against the general trend. No one, I presume, enjoys feeling different, especially when the very meaning of human life is at stake." *The Philosopher and Theology,* trans. Cécile Gilson (New

York: Random House, 1962), pp. 7–8. Gilson's point was that a Christian philosopher could not approach his special topics in any other way. Cf.: "Once you are in possession of that revelation how can you possibly philosophize as though you had never heard of it?" Gilson, *The Spirit of Mediaeval Philosophy,* trans. A. H. C. Downes (New York: Charles Scribner's Sons, 1940), p. 5.

[2] ". . . it is evident that a state exists by nature and that man is by nature a political animal." *Pol.,* 1.2,1253a2–3. Apostle trans. Cf. *E N,* 1.5,1097b11. Other references are listed in Bonitz, *Ind. Artist.,* 614a40–43. Figures for today's global population in terms of religions are only approximate, sometimes even to the millions. The most recent breakdown may be found in the editorial "A Few Figures," *Lumen Vitae,* 39 (1984): 7–9.

[3] The phrasing "their ancient rights and liberties" was used in the English *Bill of Rights* (1689). The American *Declaration of Independence* (1776) and the *Massachusetts Bill of Rights* (1780) speak of "unalienable rights." The *Virginia Bill of Rights* (1776) uses "inherent rights" and an "unalienable . . . right."

[4] "Neque enim *juris* nomine aliud significatur quam libertas, quam quisque habet facultatibus naturalibus secundum rectam rationem utendi." Thomas Hobbes, *De Cive,* 1.7. On the connection of right reason with natural law at that time, see Gregory S. Kavka, "Right Reason and Natural Law in Hobbes' *Ethics,*" *The Monist,* 66 (1983): 120–133. See also William K. Frankena, "The Ethics of Right Reason," ibid., pp. 7–8. On the topic in the present century, see Jacques Maritain, *The Rights of Man and Natural Law,* trans. Doris C. Anson (London: Charles Scribner's Sons, 1943), and the "Symposium" in the *Philosophical Review,* 64 (1955): 175–232, with the papers "Are there any Natural Rights?" (pp. 175–191), "Inalienable Rights" (pp. 192–211), and "Natural and Inalienable Rights" (pp. 212–232), by H. L. A. Hart, Stuart M. Brown, and W. K. Frankena, respectively. Maritain stresses the prominence of the right to work towards one's supernatural destiny: "The first of these rights is that of the human person to make its way towards its eternal destiny along the path which its conscience has recognized as the path indicated by God" (p. 81). The reason emphasized elsewhere by Maritain is: "The human

person is ordained directly to God as to its absolute ultimate end. Its direct ordination to God transcends every created common good—both the common good of the political society and the intrinsic common good of the universe." *The Person and the Common Good,* trans. John J. Fitzgerald (New York: Charles Scribner's Sons, 1947), p. 5. In the beatific vision, Maritain interprets the teaching of Aquinas, the direct orientation to God attains its culmination in a union in which "each blessed soul . . . becomes God intentionally" (pp. 10–11). He attributes the phrasing to Cajetan: ". . . each blesssed soul becomes God, in an intentional way, as Cajetan says, and thus enters into the uncreated society of the Divine Persons" (p. 77).

⁵Rousseau's absorption of the individual citizen into the general will is characterized by Maritain as "the finest myth of Jean-Jacques, the most religiously manufactured." *Three Reformers,* 2nd. ed. (London: Sheed & Ward, 1929), p. 134.

⁶Ronald Reagan, address, September 5, 1983; text in *New York Times,* September 6, 1983, p. 9. On the origin and bearing of the phrase "manifest destiny," see Julius W. Pratt, "The Origin of 'Manifest Destiny,'" *American Historical Review,* 32 (1927): 795–798: ". . . our destiny to overspread this entire North America with the almost miraculous progress of our population and power," p. 798.

⁷See the *Gloria* in the Latin liturgy. For the same notion in the Greek liturgy, see the Communion prayer, *Liturgy of St Basil,* in the *Library of the Greek Fathers* (Athens: Apostolic Ministry, 1978), 56: 40. For the view of the holy or numinous as an *a priori* category, see Rudolf Otto, *The Idea of the Holy,* trans. John W. Harvey (London: H. Milford, Oxford University Press, 1928), pp. 116–182. On the Aristotelian technique of focal meaning, see supra, Chapter One, nn. 20, 21, and 27.

⁸"Obviam fias illis qui, licet inscii, te expectant." *Preces,* Friday of the first week in Advent, *Liturgia Horarum,* ed. typica (Vatican City: Polyglot Press, 1974), 1: 154.

⁹Jn, 1.9; 15.4–6; Is, 26.12.

¹⁰On demonology and occult forces of evil, see Henry Ansgar Kelly, *The Devil, Demonology and Witchcraft,* 2nd ed. (Garden City, N.J.: Doubleday, 1974). James W. Boyd, *Stan and Māra* (Leiden: E. J.

Brill, 1975), with bibliography, pp. 169–177. On the analogy of Gnostic demonology with Judeo-Christian notions, and the differences from them, see Robert McLachlan Wilson, *The Gnostic Problem* (London: A. R. Mowbray, 1958), pp. 190–202. See also, on the hostile powers in Gnostic dualism, Pheme Perkins, *The Gnostic Dialogue* (New York: Paulist Press, 1980), pp. 16–17 and 170–173, with selected bibliography, pp. 218–221; Kurt Rudolph, *Gnosis,* 2nd ed., trans. ed. R. McL. Wilson (New York: Harper and Row, 1983), pp. 59–65, with selected bibliography, pp. 391–404.

[11] A survey of the "complex phenomenon of modern atheism" (p. xii) may be found in Cornelio Fabro, *God in Exile,* trans. Arthur Gibson (Westminster, Md.: Newman Press, 1968). Metaphysically, the existence of God is not immediately evident for anyone who locates the origin of human cognition in sensible things. Nor can it be deduced at once from the human notion of God. The difficulties experienced in arguments based on the idea of God, from the time of Gaunilon on, should indicate sufficiently that there is no easy demonstration of God's existence. For Aquinas's critique of the Anselmian argument, see *ST,* 1.2.1; *CG,* 1.10–11. Duns Scotus' coloring of it makes it a long and complicated reasoning process; see *Ord.,* 2.1.1–2; 2: 125–215. For a modern defense of the ontological argument, see Charles Hartshorne, *The Logic of Perfection* (La Salle, Ill.: Open Court, 1962), pp. 28–117, and *Anselm's Discovery* (La Salle, Ill.: Open Court, 1965). An interesting return to Gaunilon's original critique of it may be seen in Donald R. Gregory, "On Behalf of the Second-Rate Philosopher: A Defense of the Gaunilon Strategy against the Ontological Argument," *History of Philosophy Quarterly* 1 (1984): 49–69. The persistent dissatisfaction with the ontological argument seems enough to make one skeptical about the efficacy of any proof for God's existence based upon human ideas.

[12] See Vatican II, *Dogmatic Constitution of the Church (Lumen Gentium,* nos. 1–8. "This is the sole Church of Christ which in the Creed we profess to be one, holy, catholic and apostolic," no. 8. On its magisterium, see no. 25.

[13] See Vatican II, *Decree on Ecumenism (Unitatis Redintegratio),* nos. 1–3. With regard to the Orthodox churches, it states: "These Churches,

although separated from us, yet possess true sacraments, above all—by apostolic succession—the priesthood and the Eucharist, whereby they are still joined to us in closest intimacy," no. 15. On other "Churches and ecclesial communities," see nos. 19–23. On far eastern religions, cf. Pope John Paul II's wish "to express to you my high esteem of the millennia of precious cultural heritage and admirable traditions of which you are the guardians and living witnesses. . . . The Catholic Church is endeavoring to engage in friendly dialogue with all the great religions that have guided mankind throughout history." He stressed "the great ethical and religious visions of Buddhism and Confucianism," and urged that "our diversity in religious and ethical beliefs calls upon all of us to foster genuine fraternal dialogue and to give special consideration to what human beings have in common and to what promotes fellowship among them." "Papal Address to Non-Christian Religions," *Origins,* 14 (1984): 6. The greeting on that occasion (p. 1) was based on a saying from Confucius, quite as St. Paul (Acts 17.28) could cite pagan Greek poets. The necessity of looking upon the issues from the viewpoints of *both* sides is strongly emphasized by Jacques Scheuer, "Buddhists and Christians. Towards a Closer Encounter," *Lumen Vitae* 39 (1984): 11–27. There can be little doubt about the tendency among ecumenical people today to respect everywhere the intrinsic content of the sacred.

[14] "Pertinet autem ad christiani firmitatem non solum operari quae bona sunt, sed et tolerare quae mala sunt." Augustine, *Sermones* 46.13; in *Corpus Christianorum,* Series Latina XLI, 540.309–311. Augustine was referring to sufferings in general, but goes on to emphasize the compassion of the church towards those who err: "Tamen ipsa catholica mater, ipse pastor in ea ubique quaerit errantes, confortat infirmos, curat languidos, alligat confractos, alios ab istis, alios ab illis non se inuicem scientibus. . . . Siue dicas oues errantes a grege, siue dicas ligna praecisa de uite, nec ad reuocandas oues, nec rursus ad inserenda ligna minus idoneus est deus, quia ille summus pastor, ille uerus agricola." Ibid., 18; p. 545.449–467. Cf. "Tolerance is a paradoxical concept. It consists in permitting what one knows certainly to be an evil or an error." Giacomo Cardinal Lercaro, *Religious Tolerance in Catholic Tradition* (New York: The America Press, 1960),

p. 1. Reprinted from *Catholic Mind* 58 (1960): 12–24. Lercaro comes to grips with the question why the notion of tolerance has seemed to be a late development in Catholic thought: "The principles of tolerance should be explained not as though they represent an effort on the part of the Church to come to a compromise with the modern world. On the contrary, they represent a new development of the permanent principles of Catholicism—a development which is capable of assimilating and, at the same time, purifying what is worthwhile in modern thought" (p. 17). It has been objected that the development would not have taken place except for the seventeenth and eighteenth centuries secular thinking on human rights. History has not written its alternatives, but if that view is correct it is an added incentive for profiting from dialogue on human destiny. At any rate, in assessing the past the meanings and implications of the terms at the time have to be given careful consideration. On the meanings of "tolerance," "toleration," and "tolerationism," see Preston T. King, *Toleration* (New York: St. Martin's Press, 1976), pp. 12–13, with selected bibliography pp. 227–232. From a Protestant viewpoint, see Gustav Mensching, *Tolerance and Truth in Religion,* trans. H.-J. Klimkeit (University, Alabama: University of Alabama Press, 1971), with bibliographies pp. 196–200. On tolerance from a Marxist humanism standpoint, even during "the transitional period" (p. 56), see Paul W. Kurtz, "In Defense of Tolerance," in *Tolerance and Revolution,* ed. Paul Kurtz and Svetozar Stovjanović (Beograd: Philosophical Society of Serbia, 1970), pp. 53–60.

[15] *A Letter concerning Toleration,* in *The Second Treatise of Civil Government* and *A Letter concerning Toleration,* ed. J. W. Gough (Oxford: Basil Blackwell, 1946), p. 154.

[16] Ibid., pp. 155–156. In America even as late as 1831 Alexis de Toqueville, *Democracy in America,* (reprint; New York: Vintage Books, 1954), 1: 317, n. 3, could note the refusal to accept testimony in court from anyone who did not believe in God and in the immortality of the soul.

[17] Liberty, as Aristotle saw (*Metaph.,* 12.10,1075a19–25), involves order, insofar as free men unlike slaves do not act at random but observe what is required for the common good. Cf.: "It was never

assumed in the United States that the citizen of a free country has a right to do whatever he pleases; on the contrary, more social obligations were there imposed upon him than anywhere else." Tocqueville, 1:73. Liberty tends in this way to police itself, indicating that the greatest extension feasible is appropriate for it. Only when it violates its own intrinsic rationality is coercion in order. The suppression of human rights is in fact suicidal, for the chaos it aims to eliminate is thereby ultimately brought about, as driven home forcefully by John Paul II: "If the human person is revered and respected in his or her inviolable dignity and inalienable rights, then injustice and aggression will be seen for what they are: an arrogance that conceals within itself a certain death-wish because it subverts the balance of the natural order of fundamental equity of rights and duties, giving rise to a situation of moral chaos in which sooner or later all become victims." "The Obstacles of Peace," *Origins*, 14 (1984): 8.

¹⁸ *Metaph.*, 11.7, 1064a3–14. Cf. 11.6, 1026a19–32.

¹⁹ E.g., *Metaph.*, 1.3, 983a24–b3; 12.6, 1071b6–11.

²⁰ Cf.: "Truth can impose itself on the mind of man only in virtue of its own truth, which wins over the mind with both gentleness and power." Vatican II, *Religious Liberty*, no. 1. "One of the key truths in Catholic teaching, a truth that is contained in the word of God and constantly preached by the Fathers, is that man's response to God by faith ought to be free, and that therefore nobody is to be forced to embrace the faith against his will. The act of faith is of its very nature a free act." Ibid., no. 10.

EPILOGUE

¹ See use of this phrase in Alvin Plantinga, "The Reformed Objection to Natural Theology," *Proceedings of the American Catholic Philosophical Association* 54 (1980): 49.

² A short but well-documented account of the course taken by the main channel of Neo-Thomism may be found in Thomas J. A. Hartley, *Thomistic Revival and the Modernist Era* (Toronto: Institute of Christian Thought, St. Michael's College, 1971), pp. 30–56.

³ Aquinas, *ST*, 1.44–46; 103–105. Sometimes the term *creation* is

mistakenly held to have a temporal connotation, as though it meant that things had a temporal beginning. For Aquinas, natural reason could not demonstrate that things were created in time, but it could demonstrate that they were created, in the sense of being produced without change of any subject. On this question see William Dunphy, "Maimonides and Aquinas on Creation," in *Graceful Reason,* ed. Lloyd P. Gerson (Toronto: Pontifical Institute of Mediaeval Studies, 1983), pp. 361–379.

[4] See supra, Chapter One, nn. 19–24; Chapter Three, n. 17.

[5] In replying to the stand that wisdom based on faith cannot be a science, Aquinas shows that sacred doctrine like metaphysics is concerned with causes. But the sacred doctrine is wisdom in a higher degree than is metaphysics, because it not only deals with what is highest but also proceeds from what is highest: ". . . et multo magis haec quae non solum de altissimis, sed ex altissimis est." *In Boeth. de Trin.,* 2.2, ad 1m; ed. Bruno Decker (Leiden: E. J. Brill, 1955), p. 88.1–2. Aquinas is allowing for a science, metaphysics, that treats of divine things as its object without proceeding from divinely revealed principles. Correspondingly the modern philosophy of religion can have religious experiences and beliefs as its *object* without basing its procedure on divinely revealed articles of faith.

INDEX